EARLY LIFE

THE CAMBRIAN PERIOD

THE PREHISTORIC EARTH

Early Life:
The Cambrian Period

The First Vertebrates:
Oceans of the Paleozoic Era

March Onto Land:
The Silurian Period to the Middle Triassic Epoch

Dawn of the Dinosaur Age:
The Late Triassic & Early Jurassic Epochs

Time of the Giants:
The Middle & Late Jurassic Epochs

Last of the Dinosaurs:
The Cretaceous Period

The Rise of Mammals:
The Paleocene & Eocene Epochs

The Age of Mammals:
The Oligocene & Miocene Epochs

Primates and Human Ancestors:
The Pliocene Epoch

Early Humans:
The Pleistocene & Holocene Epochs

THE PREHISTORIC EARTH

EARLY LIFE

THE CAMBRIAN PERIOD

Thom Holmes

CHELSEA HOUSE
PUBLISHERS
An imprint of Infobase Publishing

THE PREHISTORIC EARTH: Early Life

Chelsea House
An imprint of Infobase Publishing
132 West 31st Street
New York NY 10001

Library of Congress Cataloging-in-Publication Data
Holmes, Thom.
  Early life / Thom Holmes.
      p. cm. -- (The prehistoric Earth)
  Includes bibliographical references and index.
  ISBN 978-0-8160-5957-7 (hardcover)
  1. Evolutionary paleobiology—Study and teaching—United States. 2. Fossils—Study and teaching—United States. 3. Geology, Stratigraphic—Cambrian. I. Title. II. Series.

  QE721.2.E85H65 2008
  560--dc22
              2007045328

Chelsea House books are available at special discounts when purchased in bulk quantities for businesses, associations, institutions, or sales promotions. Please call our Special Sales Department in New York at (212) 967-8800 or (800) 322-8755.

You can find Chelsea House on the World Wide Web at http://www.chelseahouse.com

Text design by Kerry Casey
Cover design by Salvatore Luongo

Printed in the United States of America

Bang NMSG 10 9 8 7 6 5 4 3 2 1

This book is printed on acid-free paper.

All links and Web addresses were checked and verified to be correct at the time of publication. Because of the dynamic nature of the Web, some addresses and links may have changed since publication and may no longer be valid.

CONTENTS

PREFACE

To be curious about the future one must know something about the past.

Humans have been recording events in the world around them for about 5,300 years. That is how long it has been since the Sumerian people, in a land that today is southern Iraq, invented the first known written language. Writing allowed people to document what they saw happening around them. The written word gave a new permanency to life. Language, and writing in particular, made history possible.

History is a marvelous human invention, but how do people know about things that happened before language existed? Or before humans existed? Events that took place before human record keeping began are called *prehistory*. Prehistoric life is, by its definition, any life that existed before human beings existed and were able to record for posterity what was happening in the world around them.

Prehistory is as much a product of the human mind as history. Scientists who specialize in unraveling clues of prehistoric life are called paleontologists. They study life that existed before human history, often hundreds of thousands and millions of years in the past. Their primary clues come from fossils of animals and plants and from geologic evidence about Earth's topography and climate. Through the skilled and often imaginative interpretation of fossils, paleontologists are able to reconstruct the appearance, lifestyle, environment, and relationships of ancient life-forms. While paleontology is grounded in a study of prehistoric life, it draws on many other sciences to complete an accurate picture of the past. Information from the fields of biology, zoology, geology, chemistry, meteorology, and even astrophysics is called into play to help the paleontologist view the past through the lens of today's knowledge.

If a writer were to write a history of all sports, would it be enough to write only about table tennis? Certainly not. On the shelves of bookstores and libraries, however, we find just such a slanted perspective toward the story of the dinosaurs. Dinosaurs have captured our imagination at the expense of many other equally fascinating, terrifying, and unusual creatures. Dinosaurs were not alone in the pantheon of prehistoric life, but it is rare to find a book that also mentions the many other kinds of life that came before and after the dinosaurs.

The Prehistoric Earth is a series that explores the evolution of life from its earliest forms 3.5 billion years ago until the emergence of modern humans some 300,000 years ago. Four volumes in the series trace the story of the dinosaurs. Six other volumes are devoted to the kinds of animals that evolved before, during, and after the reign of the dinosaurs. *The Prehistoric Earth* covers the early explosion of life in the oceans; the invasion of the land by the first land animals; the rise of fishes, amphibians, reptiles, mammals, and birds; and the emergence of modern humans.

The Prehistoric Earth series is written for readers in high school. Based on the latest scientific findings in paleontology, *The Prehistoric Earth* is the most comprehensive and up-to-date series of its kind for this age group.

The first volume in the series, *Early Life*, offers foundational information about geologic time, Earth science, fossils, the classification of organisms, and evolution. This volume also begins the chronological exploration of fossil life that explodes with the incredible life-forms of the Precambrian and Cambrian Periods, more than 500 million years ago.

The remaining nine volumes in the series can be read chronologically. Each volume covers a specific geologic time period and describes the major forms of life that lived at that time. The books also trace the geologic forces and climate changes that affected the evolution of life through the ages. Readers of *The Prehistoric Earth* will see the whole picture of prehistoric life take shape. They will learn about forces that affect life on Earth, the directions that life can sometimes take, and ways in which all life-forms depend on each other in the environment. Along the way, readers also will meet many of the scientists who have made remarkable discoveries about the prehistoric Earth.

The language of science is used throughout this series, with ample definition and an extensive glossary provided in each volume. Important concepts involving geology, evolution, and the lifestyles of early animals are presented logically, step by step. Illustrations, photographs, tables, and maps reinforce and enhance the books' presentation of the story of prehistoric life.

While telling the story of prehistoric life, the author hopes that many readers will be sufficiently intrigued to continue studies on their own. For this purpose, throughout each volume, special "Think About It" features offer additional insights or interesting exercises for readers who wish to explore certain topics. Each book in the series also provides a chapter-by-chapter bibliography of books, journals, and Web sites.

Only about one-tenth of 1 percent of all species of prehistoric animals are known from fossils. A multitude of discoveries remain to be made in the field of paleontology. It is with earnest, best wishes that I hope that some of these discoveries will be made by readers inspired by this series.

—Thom Holmes
Jersey City, New Jersey

ACKNOWLEDGMENTS

I would like to thank the many dedicated and hardworking people at Chelsea House. A special debt of gratitude goes to my editors, Shirley White, Brian Belval and Frank Darmstadt, for their support and guidance in conceiving and making *The Prehistoric Earth* a reality. Frank was instrumental in fine-tuning the features of the series as well as accepting my ambitious plan for creating a comprehensive reference for students. Brian greatly influenced the development of the color illustration program and supported my efforts to integrate the work of some of the best artists in the field, most notably John Sibbick, whose work appears throughout the set. Shirley's excellent questions about the science behind the books greatly contributed to the readability of the results. The excellent copyediting of Mary Ellen Kelly was both thoughtful and vital to shaping the final manuscript. I thank Mary Ellen for her patience as well as her valuable review and suggestions that help make the books a success.

I am privileged to have worked with some of the brightest minds in paleontology on this series. Ted Daeschler of the Academy of Natural Sciences in Philadelphia reviewed the draft of *Early Life* and made many important suggestions that affected the course of the work. Ted also wrote the Foreword for the volume.

In many ways, a set of books such as this requires years of preparation. Some of the work is educational, and I owe much gratitude to Dr. Peter Dodson of the University of Pennsylvania for his gracious and inspiring tutelage over the years. Another dimension of preparation requires experience digging fossils, and for giving me these opportunities, I thank my friends and colleagues who have taken me into the field with them, including Phil Currie, Rodolfo Coria, Matthew Lammana, and Ruben Martinez. Finally comes the work needed to put thoughts down on paper and complete the draft of a book, a process that always takes many more hours than I plan on. I thank Anne for bearing with my constant state of busy-ness and for helping me remember the important things in life. You are an inspiration to me. I also thank my daughter Shaina, the genius in the family and another inspiration, for always being supportive and humoring her father's obsession with prehistoric life.

FOREWORD

The history of life on Earth is a magnificent consequence of evolutionary processes played out over billions of years. Collecting evidence and using science to reconstruct the past and connect it to the present is the job of a paleontologist. Part of the excitement of paleontology comes from understanding how we know what we know and why there is a lot more to learn. Paleontology is a relatively young science and clearly in a phase of ongoing discoveries from all segments of geologic time and biological diversity.

This book, *Early Life*, is part of a series called *The Prehistoric Earth*. The series is a state-of-the-art review of the current understanding of many aspects of paleontology. If you are like most people, you are already familiar with one or two groups of animals from the prehistoric past. These books will provide the opportunity to build your knowledge base and get a better overall look at the amazing history of life. I think you will agree that a view of the larger picture helps us to appreciate and better understand the more-often-encountered information on dinosaurs, Ice Age mammals, or human evolution.

Paleontology is not a disparate series of facts about fossil plants and animals. A true understanding of paleontology requires building a foundation of general principles and processes that give you a more thorough appreciation of the fossil record. In *Early Life*, Thom Holmes provides an explanation of some of the important building blocks of paleontology. As you read the first three sections in this book—Reconstructing Earth's Past, How Prehistoric Life Is Revealed, and How Life Develops and Its Classification—you will find the general ideas and principles that should be firmly understood as you explore further in *The Prehistoric Earth*. These three sections will introduce you to the physical processes that determine

13

the changing conditions for life on Earth. The author also explains the nature of the processes that profoundly effect what we find in the fossil record as it is preserved in sedimentary rocks. He explains other important aspects of fossils, including how rocks and fossils can be used to measure time, the processes of extinction and evolution, and the way that prehistoric life is classified.

In Section Four, Early Life, Thom Holmes provides an up-to-date assessment of the origin of life and its simple beginnings. Due to the fragility of the earliest forms of life and the nature of the rock record from the first several billion years of Earth's history, the fossil record of the small, simple life-forms from the Precambrian Period is quite limited. Though we still have a lot to learn about the first four billion years of Earth history, the author has provided a context for the events that led up to the monumental diversification of life in the Cambrian Period. The fascinating diversity of life that is revealed in the Burgess Shale and other Cambrian fossil treasure troves set the stage for understanding the origins of many of the animal groups that we know today. The exploration of the varied and strange animals from the Burgess Shale illustrates the ability of scientific discourse to refine ideas as new information is presented.

This is an exciting time to learn about paleontology. There are many new discoveries from throughout geologic time, new interpretations of previously studied fossils, and new techniques for pulling more information from the fossil record. Studies in evolutionary biology are providing better ideas of the mechanisms of evolution. Geological studies are refining our understanding of the physical, ecological, and temporal framework for the history of life.

Enjoy reading *Early Life*, and keep its big ideas with you as you continue to learn about paleontology.

—Dr. Ted Daeschler
Academy of Natural Sciences
Philadelphia, Pennsylvania

INTRODUCTION

This is a book about the earliest forms of life that evolved on our planet. Earth is about 4.5 billion years old. Life on Earth, however, did not exist from the outset of the planet's existence. It took about 500 million years before conditions on the planet could support life of any kind. That is about when the first single-celled organisms, probably bacteria and then algae, evolved and led the way to the extraordinary cavalcade of organisms that have walked Earth's stage ever since. This volume of *The Prehistoric Earth* is about the first burst of life that is found in the fossil record, extending from the first signs of life in the Precambrian Period to the end of the Cambrian Period about 488 million years ago.

This volume has two distinct purposes. The first purpose is to provide background on the science of paleontology and fossils. Sections One, Two, and Three introduce several essential concepts that will help the reader understand geologic forces shaping the Earth, concepts of geologic time, evolution, and the ways in which scientists classify living organisms.

The second purpose of this volume is to provide a detailed look at the first life-forms to evolve on our planet. This information is covered in Section 4.

PALEONTOLOGY: THE SCIENCE OF PAST LIFE

Paleontology is the study of prehistoric life, primarily through the interpretation of fossils. When we read about dinosaurs, wooly mammoths, trilobites, cave people, and other extinct organisms, we are sharing the knowledge gained through the work of paleontologists.

Paleontology may be the study of extinct organisms going back to the earliest stages of life on Earth; but as a science, paleontology is relatively new when we compare it to mathematics, physics, and astronomy. Paleontology blossomed during the middle of the nineteenth century as the discovery of fossils around the world began to attract serious scientific scrutiny.

Paleontology could not have existed in its present form, however, without several important breakthroughs in nineteenth-century science. First, there had to be some agreement on the age of the Earth and the length of time that it took for geologic changes to take place. The forces that change the Earth over eons and the groundbreaking concept of geologic time first stated by British naturalist Sir Charles Lyell are the subjects of Chapters 1 and 2. These geologic ideas also led to an understanding of the nature of fossils and what they are, which is the subject of Chapter 3.

Another nineteenth-century concept that was vital to the fledgling science of paleontology was that of extinction, the idea that some lines of organisms could perish over time. Had scientists not accepted this idea, the animals discovered as fossils could not have been understood in their proper biological context. In the 3.5 billion years that life has existed on Earth, even the most resilient lines of multicelled organisms have existed for only brief windows of geologic time. The dinosaurs lasted for only 4 percent of the total time that Earth has been in existence. Trilobites occupied 7 percent of this time and the birds (today's descendents of dinosaurs) only about 6 percent. By comparison, humans are truly newcomers. Even if we include ancestral forms of hominoids that led to modern humans, man and woman have only been around for one-half of 1 percent of the time that Earth has been a planet. How long will it be until we face the inevitability of human extinction? Will we know when it is coming? The concept of extinction and what it means is covered in Chapter 4.

Another core concept that governs the work of paleontologists is that of evolution. Charles Darwin (1809–1882) was instrumental in proposing a concept of evolution through natural selection that continues to this day to shape our understanding of life and how it changes over time. Since the time of Darwin, the discovery of DNA and the use of computers to conduct analyses of the evolutionary relationships between organisms has provided much sought after proof not only that evolution occurs, but also of the critical factors that affect it. The concept of evolution is key to an understanding of prehistoric life because it tells us who is related to whom and how changes in the environment affect the course of a species' existence. It also provides the basis for a system of classifying all life-forms. Evolution and classification are the subjects of Chapters 5 and 6.

THE EXPLORATION OF EARLY LIFE

An understanding of early life and how it evolved continues to be one of the most fascinating disciplines within paleontology. While fossil evidence for the first single-celled organisms exists, the question of how they evolved has been a question for biochemists and others who experiment with models of the primordial Earth. This is coupled with evidence about the early Earth's atmosphere, changes affecting the chemistry of the oceans, and a balance of elements that led to the first organisms. Life's beginnings, from the appearance of early colonies of algae to the first definitive multicelled ocean creatures known as the Vendian fauna, are covered in Chapter 7.

The conclusion of *Early Life* covers one of the most extraordinary periods in the evolution of life on Earth, the Cambrian. It was the time of the "biological big bang," a relatively short span of time during which nearly all basic forms of animal life that still exist first appear in the fossil record of the ancient oceans. It was a time of strange marine creatures that appear more like aliens from another planet. The Cambrian Period was the time of the first predators and of a biological arms race that pitted elegant strategies for defense against increasingly efficient means of attack. The Cambrian Period also gave us the first chordates, animals with a notochord, a significant biological milestone that led directly to the evolution of vertebrates. The roots of all land animals are in the Cambrian Period.

Many discoveries recounted in this book could not have been explained even five years ago. The mysteries of Cambrian life are an important part of today's paleontological research. Discoveries about this critical period in the evolution of life are actively being made at fossil sites as distant from one another as western Canada, China, and Greenland. *Early Life* draws from the latest research to tell the compelling story of early life and its enormous importance to understanding other species of life that have evolved since.

SECTION ONE:
RECONSTRUCTING EARTH'S PAST

1

THE CHANGING EARTH

We usually think of the Earth as a stable, unchanging entity. This impression is sometimes shaken by the real-life drama of a natural catastrophe. An earthquake might propel a deadly tsunami across a vast expanse of ocean. An erupting volcano might pour hot ash and lava over a nearby town. These and other disasters are a reminder that Earth is a restless planet. Powerful forces are always at work in the world, making slow but continuous changes that occasionally explode as a stark reminder that life exists at the whim of geologic events. The constantly changing nature of the Earth underscores a simple truism: Life is ultimately made possible and shaped by the habitats and conditions provided by the planet.

Before considering the development and history of life, it is important to understand the physical forces that make life possible. Earth science provides clues to understanding the age of prehistoric **organisms**, the environment in which they thrived, and the manner in which their **species** lived and died. This chapter introduces the composition of the Earth and the physical forces that account for its constantly changing structure. Of special interest is the nature of Earth's surface, how it changes over many millions of years, and how these changes create challenges to the development of life.

FORMATION OF THE EARTH

The universe, with its trillions of stars and billions of galaxies, began about 15 billion years ago. The universe came into being because of an enormous explosion—a really "**big bang**," as the event has been called. But it was not like any explosion ever witnessed by humans. Prior to the big bang, all matter and energy that existed were concentrated in a finite point in space. With the big bang, all matter began to expand away from this point, spewing out in all directions. All of the elementary particles of the embryonic universe were thrown outward in every direction, forming an ever-expanding realm that defines the reaches of space. Time itself, and space, came into existence because of the big bang, along with the fundamental laws of physics that govern the universe: gravity, electromagnetism, and the building blocks of atoms.

Following the big bang, cosmic particles were not spread evenly across the universe. Much of the debris began to clump together as a result of gravitation. Clouds of dust and gas formed great spiral galaxies. The matter within these galaxies condensed further as the universe cooled. Such increasingly dense masses of cosmic matter began to create stronger gravitational fields of their own. When these nuclear reactions occurred in a highly concentrated manner, stars were often formed. Our own Sun is one such star. Meanwhile, other cosmic debris continued to clump together, forming planets, comets, asteroids, and other objects found in space.

The big bang was so powerful that the universe is still expanding because of it. Every second, the galaxies grow farther apart. In the farthest reaches of the universe, scientists have also detected faint residue of the original explosion in the form of background radiation.

Earth began to form about 4.5 billion years ago from the accumulation of small, cold pieces of metals and rocks that orbited the Sun. As the planet grew larger, it also became hotter as several natural forces released energy: the collision of space rocks into the Earth, the compaction of the Earth due to its increasingly powerful gravitational field, and the radioactive decay of elements found within its rocks, such as uranium.

The temperature of the formative Earth grew so high that it melted the metals found in its rocks. These molten metals were pulled inward toward the planet's center to form the **core** and **mantle**. The outer surface, or **crust**, did not begin to form until between 4.3 billion and 4.4 billion years ago. This was a convulsive and violent time in Earth's history. Fueled by the molten metals of its interior, volcanic activity spurted great quantities of water vapor and other gases into the atmosphere. The surface of the planet was covered with oceans of red-hot lava. The crust probably formed, broke apart, and reformed many times during this span until the tremendous heat and volcanism slowed enough for large parts of the crust to cool and stabilize. The vast quantities of water vapor found in the early atmosphere of the planet then began to condense and to rain down on the planet in vast quantities. These rains formed the first true oceans beginning about 4 billion years ago. The planet continued to expel its gases through heat and volcanic activity, and the oceans became salty from chlorine and sodium released by volcanic gases and the weathering of minerals from the Earth's surface. The stage was set for the emergence of life.

STRUCTURE OF THE EARTH

It was not until the twentieth century that the structure of the Earth was well understood. Before that, the interior of the planet was as puzzling a mystery as the far reaches of outer space. There were many grand theories about the composition of the Earth, ranging from it being all liquid to all solid to something in between. What made this puzzle doubly fascinating was that nobody could travel deep inside the Earth to discover what it was made of.

In 1864, French author Jules Verne (1828–1905) published his famous adventure novel *A Journey to the Center of the Earth*. Verne was an early writer of speculative fiction, also called science fiction. Verne was well educated in science and especially knowledgeable about geology, geography, and astronomy. In *A Journey to the Center of the Earth*, he took advantage of public curiosity about Earth science with a thrilling story of descent into the deepest reaches of the planet. But even the greatest geologists of the time had no solid evidence for the nature of Earth's interior. In his novel, Verne's band of European explorers traveled down through an inactive volcanic crater in Iceland that served as a portal to the wonders below. Descending over 100 miles (about 161 km) in this fictitious trek, the explorers found that the interior of the planet was full of marvelous caverns, breathable air, underground oceans, sea monsters, graveyards of prehistoric animals, giant land-dwelling "shark crocodiles," and gorillas that were 14 feet (4.3 m) tall. Although Verne's view of Earth's interior from the vantage point of 1864 had little resemblance to reality, his fanciful tale filled a void not yet addressed by leading geologists of his time.

Early scientific debate about the structure of the Earth began about 75 years before Verne published *A Journey to the Center of the Earth*. Early geologists focused on features of the planet that could be seen on the surface. Two eighteenth-century geologists, Abraham Gottlob Werner (1750–1817) of Germany and James Hutton (1726–1797) of Scotland, were early advocates of opposing points of view about Earth's composition. Werner believed that Earth had once been covered by a vast ocean of deep water, heavy with sediment. He theorized that over time, as the ocean diminished, sediment was deposited in equal layers all over the globe. Followers of Werner were known as Neptunists after the Roman god of the ocean, Neptune. Neptunists believed that Earth was composed of uniform layers of rock deposits that resembled the rings of an onion.

Hutton's observations about Earth's crust were more astute than Werner's. Hutton recognized the difference between **sedimentary rock**, formed by the forces of **erosion** and by deposition, and **igneous rock**, which had at one time been molten. Hutton noticed that layers of sedimentary rock were sometimes upturned or shot through with a vein of igneous rock, such as granite. He theorized that these dramatic changes to the crust of the Earth could only have been caused by tremendous subterranean forces of heat and pressure. Accordingly, Hutton dubbed his idea the Plutonian theory after Pluto, the Roman god of the underworld.

Hutton's views eventually won out over Werner's because of a debate over the origin of basalt, a type of igneous rock. Basalt is commonly found in the crust of the Earth, including the ocean floor. After molten basalt was seen for the first time streaming out of an active volcano, the argument swung to the side of the Plutonists.

With the coming of the twentieth century, geologists were still hindered by the inability to travel deep into the Earth to observe and describe the internal structure of the planet with accuracy. Fortunately, with the development of new scientific instrumentation, it became possible to study the interior of the Earth using indirect methods. The branch of geology that deals with the composition and structure of the Earth is **geophysics**.

The best evidence for the structure of Earth's interior comes from the study of seismic waves, the vibrations caused by earthquakes. The **seismograph** is a scientific instrument used to detect and measure seismic waves. The first modern seismograph was invented in 1880 by British geologist and mining engineer John Milne (1850–1913). By the early twentieth century, a worldwide network of seismographs enabled geologists to use seismic wave measurements to reveal the true nature of Earth's interior.

The basic purpose of a seismograph is to measure the strength of an earthquake. This is done by recording the magnitude of shock waves emanating from a tremor. These measurements provide data for sizing up and locating layers of rock within the Earth.

The seismograph is used to study a phenomenon known as **seismic reflection**. When an earthquake takes place, seismic shock waves are generated downward from the quake's **epicenter** to the interior of the planet. Some of these waves bounce back off layers of rock and can be detected by a seismograph. The seismograph shows how long it takes for a wave to travel down to the rock layer and reflect back. The depth of the rock layer can then be calculated based on this round trip from the epicenter of the earthquake to the location of the seismograph.

Seismographs are also used to detect the boundaries between different rock layers through a process called **seismic refraction**. Just as light bends when it passes through glass lenses of different thickness, so, too, do seismic waves bend when they travel through rock layers of different thickness. When the shock waves from a single earthquake are divided and refracted over great distances, geologists can use seismograph readings to detect the boundaries between rock layers. These measurements also indicate places in Earth's interior that are more solid than others.

In 1914, German geologist Beno Gutenberg (1889–1960) became the first scientist to use distant seismic recordings of earthquakes to suggest that the Earth had a solid core. Danish geologist Inge Lehmann (1888–1993) perfected these measurements, and by 1939 she confirmed the presence of an inner core. Following this discovery and the availability of increasingly accurate seismographs, geologists were able to form a highly accurate picture of the inside of the Earth.

Seismic waves are not the only available clues to the makeup of Earth's interior. In addition to seismic readings, several other indirect techniques are used to study the composition of the Earth.

- The study of gravity and the use of the **gravity meter** determines variations in rock density.
- The **magnetometer** measures the strength of Earth's magnetic field. Because metals are good conductors of electromagnetic energy, and silicate rocks are not, local anomalies—irregularities and differences—in magnetic fields reveal something about variations in rock type.
- Studying Earth's heat flow also reveals something about what is hidden inside the planet. High heat flow measured at the crust can indicate the presence of molten **magma**, the rise of a section of mantle below a thin layer of crust, or even the presence of highly radioactive igneous rock.

All of these indirect methods of studying Earth's interior clearly reveal that the planet is not a solid globe. It is composed of three major zones of material, both liquid and solid: the core, the mantle, and the crust. The major regions of Earth's interior have the following features:

Inner Solid Core. Earth's core has two parts, the inner and outer cores. At the center of the Earth is the inner core. The inner core is extraordinarily dense and made up primarily of iron. Geophysicists base this conclusion on several lines of reasoning. Calculations made using Newton's law of gravitational attraction suggest that the core is about as dense as iron. This suggestion is confirmed by measurements of Earth's magnetic field, the extraordinary strength of which requires that the inner core be made of an excellent electrical conductor, such as iron. The density of the core is also similar to that of iron-based meteorites, which are probably similar to the formative materials that once came together to form the Earth. While being dense, the inner core is also hot. Radioactive elements mingling within the core slowly decay and emit great amounts of heat energy. The temperature of the inner core is more than 10,000°F (5,538°C). This would normally be hot enough to melt any metal to a liquid. But the tremendous weight that the Earth exerts on the inner core keeps it solid. This heat is the primary driving force behind the large-scale movements of the continents on Earth's surface. The solid inner core is about 730 miles (1,175 km) thick.

Outer Liquid Core. Surrounding the inner core is the outer core, also made up largely of iron and nickel. The inner core is so hot that it melts the outer core. The inner core floats inside the outer core. The liquid outer core is about 1,350 miles (2,173 km) thick.

Mantle. The mantle surrounds the core of the Earth and lies between the core and the outer surface or crust. Like the white part of an apple, the mantle makes up most of Earth's mass—about 80 percent. The mantle is 1,740 miles (2,800 km) thick and made up of semimolten metals and other minerals. The hot mantle is always on the move like a huge ring of steaming oatmeal. This "oatmeal" is called magma and is the stuff behind volcanic eruptions and other disruptions of Earth's surface. The slow movement of the mantle and its contact with the outer crust of the Earth is the cause of many changes on the surface.

Crust. The crust is the exterior surface of the Earth. It is cooler than the interior of the planet but subject to the heat and movement of matter beneath its surface. The crust includes dry land as well as the floors of oceans and lakes. The crust is also cracked and can break apart, and it is much thinner than the mantle. The crust is only about three miles (5 km) thick under the oceans but varies widely in thickness on dry land. On average, it is about 18 miles

Internal Structure of Earth

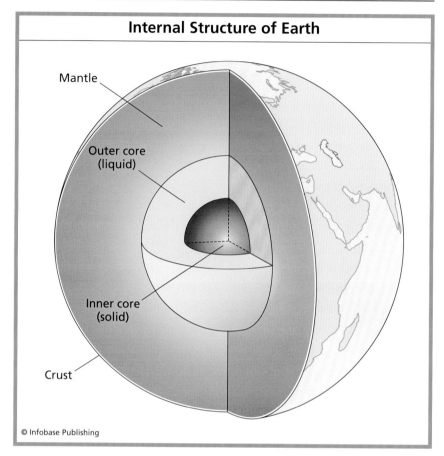

Mantle

Outer core
(liquid)

Inner core
(solid)

Crust

© Infobase Publishing

If cut open like a piece of fruit, the Earth would reveal several layers in cross-section, including the inner core, outer core, mantle, and crust.

(about 30 km) thick. Beneath mountains, such as the Alps, it can be as thick as 60 miles (about 100 km).

The heat that comes from the inner core of the Earth is the catalyst for changes that affect the mantle and crust every day. This heat causes the mantle to circulate. In turn, the mantle moves the continents, forms mountains by pushing up the crust, causes earthquakes, and triggers volcanic eruptions.

FORCES CHANGING THE EARTH

The surface of the Earth may seem stable and solid, but it is actually changing all the time. There is evidence of these changes all around us. Mountains, gullies, and canyons are the result of changes that have taken place over long periods of time. Glaciers make deep gouges in the surface of the Earth as they grow and recede with changes in temperature. The paths of rivers, the increase and decrease in size of lakes, and the constant beating on the shoreline by ocean waves all make changes to Earth's crust that are easily seen.

The Earth is also subject to more violent and immediate changes. Earthquakes can shake the ground and rattle buildings into rubble. Volcanoes can explode with mighty force, scorching the ground for miles, killing wildlife, and raining down a firestorm of ash. Living things have no control over these phenomena. Life can persist only if the changing Earth makes it possible.

What makes the Earth so restless? Two main forces lead to all of the changes in Earth's surface: heat and gravity.

Heat from outside the Earth comes from the Sun. Heat causes temperature changes on Earth and sets many processes in motion. Heat influences the circulation of wind over land and oceans. Heat also causes water from rivers, lakes, and oceans to **evaporate** and rise as a gas into the atmosphere. This moisture in the air eventually leads to **precipitation** in the form of rain, snow, hail, or sleet. The effects of wind, precipitation, and air temperature slowly cause erosion and other local changes to the surface of the Earth.

Heat not only comes from the Sun, it also comes from deep within the Earth. The planet's core is like a constantly burning furnace. Its radiant heat energy works from within over long periods of time, making changes that are geographically widespread and often on a massive scale.

Gravity also plays an important role in shaping the surface of the Earth. Gravity is a force, and a large amount of gravity is found in any large, body in space, such as a planet, moon, or sun. Gravity is what keeps objects on the surface of the Earth. The pull of Earth's gravity holds Earth's Moon in its orbit. The Sun has its own powerful gravitational pull that keeps its planets orbiting around it.

Gravity shapes the surface of the Earth in many ways. Gravity makes rain fall to the ground. Gravity causes rivers to flow downstream and the oceans to shift with the tides. Gravity also makes objects—falling leaves, crumbling dirt, and blowing sand, for example—fall to the ground. The movement of water, especially in rivers, lakes, and oceans, causes dramatic and visible changes to the ground. A river slowly but constantly changes its course, depositing mud in some places, eroding mud away in others. The same mud that is carried away by the river may also be deposited downstream, building up layers of sand and dirt where there was little before. Driven by the force of gravity, flowing water is a powerful sculptor of the Earth. These changes affect the environment of the plants and animals that live near water.

Movement of Earth's Crust

Earth's crust is moving. The movement is slight—only about two inches (5 cm) per year—but over long periods of time this movement can produce dramatic changes to the surface of the planet. Volcanoes, earthquakes, and mountains are all caused by movement in the crust.

Earth's surface is made up of many large slabs of crust that ride on top of Earth's molten mantle. These slabs are called **tectonic plates.** There are a dozen or more tectonic plates that interlock to make up the fragmented crust of the Earth.

What causes the plates to move is the underlying mantle on which they rest. The mantle is heated by Earth's core, which in turn creates the thick, molten magma. The hottest magma rises through the mantle, comes in contact with the underside of the crust, and then slowly falls again as it cools. The mantle is constantly circulating magma through this cycle of **convection** currents caused by heat.

Tectonic plates ride on top of the mantle and are moved in different directions by the convection currents of the mantle. It is as though many conveyor belts of different sizes and directions are rolling against the tectonic plates at all times. But where can the plates go if they are pushed?

To picture the major tectonic plates and their motion, imagine the surface of the Earth without oceans. The major plates lie partly

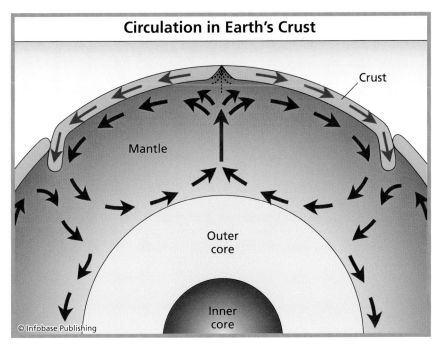

Circulation in Earth's Crust

Crust

Mantle

Outer core

Inner core

© Infobase Publishing

Circulating currents of hot magma in Earth's mantle are a primary cause for the movement of tectonic plates. The hottest magma rises through the mantle, comes in contact with the underside of the crust, and then slowly falls again as it cools. The mantle is constantly circulating magma through this cycle of convection currents caused by heat.

on dry land and partly under the oceans. Most of the boundaries where the plates meet are under the oceans. Sometimes, magma bubbles up from the mantle and quickly hardens, adding to the crust. This seeping magma builds up over time, forming undersea mountain ranges known as **oceanic ridges**. The slow but constant buildup of these ridges slowly pushes the two plates apart.

Oceanic ridges run down the center of the world's largest oceans. The longest is the mid-ocean ridge that extends nearly 40,000 miles (64,000 km), connecting many of the world's oceans. Oceanic ridges are one of Earth's most extensive geologic features.

The largest mountain in the world begins on the ocean floor. It is Mount Kea, on the island of Hawaii, in the Pacific Ocean. Mount Kea is 33,474 feet (10,203 m) tall, with 13,680 feet (4,170 m) rising above sea level. This exceeds the tallest mountain found solely on

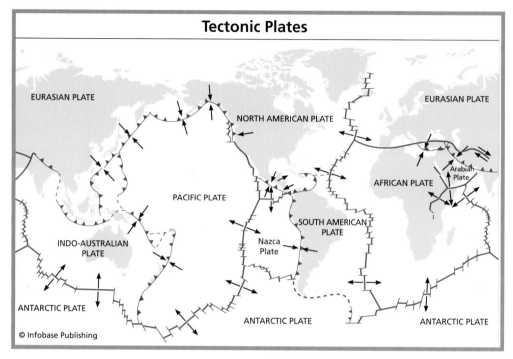

Tectonic Plates

EURASIAN PLATE

NORTH AMERICAN PLATE

EURASIAN PLATE

Arabian Plate

AFRICAN PLATE

PACIFIC PLATE

SOUTH AMERICAN PLATE

INDO-AUSTRALIAN PLATE

Nazca Plate

ANTARCTIC PLATE

ANTARCTIC PLATE

ANTARCTIC PLATE

© Infobase Publishing

Major and minor tectonic plates make up the outer surface of Earth.

land—Mount Everest in Nepal—by 4,439 feet (1,353 m). The mid-ocean ridge is made up of many more spectacular undersea mountains, dramatic evidence of upheaval in Earth's long history.

Tectonic plates may also collide with great force under the ocean. Instead of forming a ridge, one plate is shoved underneath the other into the hot mantle below. This forms a deep, linear depression on the seafloor called a trench or **subduction zone**. As the one plate is forced down, it is melted by the intense heat. This can cause violent eruptions from inside the Earth, resulting in volcanic explosions and the formation of mountain ranges. The Andes Mountains were formed this way, from underneath an ancient ocean. Some of the most significant changes in tectonic plates, therefore, take place on the ocean floor. Oceanic plates are constantly moving—spreading out from some collision points, sinking at some others, and being regenerated over time.

Other dramatic changes to Earth's surface are caused by the movement of tectonic plates. When two plates slide past each other

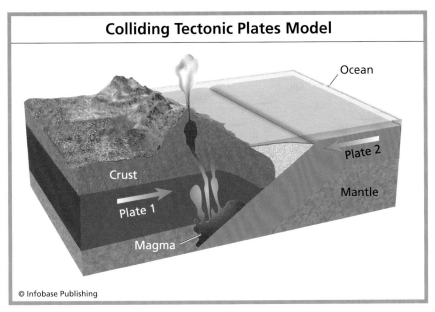

Colliding Tectonic Plates Model

Ocean

Plate 2

Crust

Mantle

Plate 1

Magma

© Infobase Publishing

Tectonic plates may grind past each other with great force. As one plate is forced down, it is melted by intense heat. This can cause violent eruptions from inside Earth, sometimes resulting in volcanic explosions.

in different directions, they create a fault line. This movement is the cause of earthquakes.

Sometimes, when two plates collide, neither one is shoved down into the mantle. The edges of the plates may be thrust one over the other, slowly building a thick, complex pile of crust material. This gradually forms a continental collision, the early stage of the formation of an oceanic ridge. The Alps were formed in this way.

It is also possible that two plates might move away from each other. This causes a gap between the plates called a **rift**. If given enough time, a rift may become so deep and long that it will cause a new ocean to form, and possibly a new continent.

While the slow movement of tectonic plates is not perceptible without the use of high-precision scientific instruments, moving plates have caused dramatic changes to the surface of the Earth over many millions of years. One might not be able to feel the constant grinding and bumping that goes on when these massive chunks of Earth knock into each other, but the effects will influence the

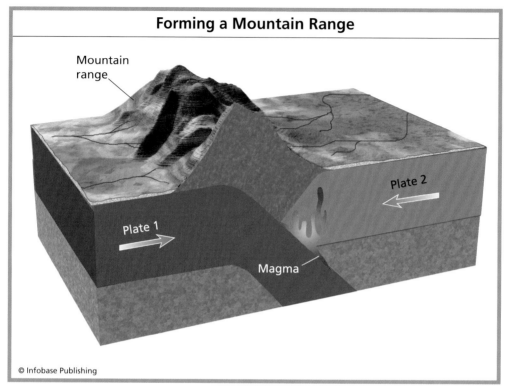

Forming a Mountain Range

Mountain range

Plate 2

Plate 1

Magma

© Infobase Publishing

The collision of two tectonic plates may cause the crust above to thrust upward, forming mountain ranges.

survival and continuance of life for many millions of years to come. How momentous can these changes be? A look at tectonic-plate movements of the prehistoric Earth provides conclusive evidence.

The Drifting Continents

All of the individual forces that change the face of the Earth are overshadowed by their combined effect on the movement of the continents. Since the formation of the Earth, the crust has continued to change its size and location due to the action of plate tectonics. The movement of the continents, also called **continental drift**, was understood during only the past 90 years. Before that time, the idea that Earth's crust was made up of individually moving plates was thought absurd by most scientists.

Anyone who has examined a world map can see that the outlines of certain continents seem to match up like the pieces of a jigsaw puzzle. It is obvious that the east coasts of North and South America closely match the west coasts of Europe and Africa. When put together, they appear to have been parts of a single landmass that must have broken apart. But how could this be possible? It should not be surprising that this observation had been made for a few centuries, ever since the first world maps were created. But nobody could imagine that the continents were moving at all. What kind of forces exist that can move continents?

Alfred Wegener (1880–1930), a German meteorologist, was the first scientist to seriously investigate the idea of moving continents. Wegener was well ahead of his time in 1912 when he proposed his theory of continental drift. What made his thinking unique

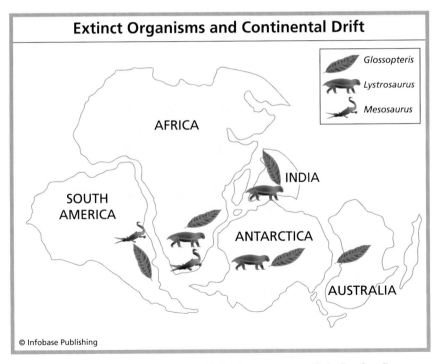

One form of proof for continental drift is the presence of similar fossils on continents that are now widely separated by oceans. At one time, prehistoric creatures wandered freely over land masses that were joined together.

was that Wegener based his theory on more than just the shape of the continents. True, in taking a close look at South America and Africa, Wegener noted that the two had remarkably similar geologic features. He also saw, however, that many similar plant and animal **fossils** were found in both places. A fossil is a physical trace of prehistoric life. Wegener felt that it would have been impossible for these plants and animals to find their way across a vast ocean. To Wegener, the answer seemed clear. He theorized that Africa and South America, along with the rest of the continents, were once joined as a "super continent," which he called *Pangaea*. Over a long period of time, long before the existence of people, Pangaea gradually broke apart and spread across the globe. As further evidence of this, Wegener noted that it was possible to find fossils of tropical plants in frozen Antarctica. He postulated that this would not have been possible unless this frigid continent from the bottom of the world had once been a part of a warmer **climate** farther north. An abundance of fossil evidence now links separate continents.

Wegener published his astonishing theory in a book titled *The Origin of Continents and Oceans* (1915). Although he was the first to propose that the continents were slowly moving over time, Wegener could not provide a convincing explanation for how this happened. No scientist by Wegener's time had yet identified natural forces great enough to cause such massive movements of Earth's crust. What Wegener lacked was proof about plate tectonics and how the fragmented crust of the Earth was always in motion. His inability to provide a plausible explanation that could be proved by other scientists led to widespread ridicule of his theory. One scientific rival, Dr. Rollin T. Chamberlin (1881–1948) of the University of Chicago, lambasted Wegener, saying his hypothesis was, " . . . of the footloose type, in that it takes considerable liberty with our globe, and is less bound by restrictions or tied down by awkward, ugly facts than most of its rival theories."

Still, Wegener believed strongly in his idea and spent the rest of his life seeking more evidence to prove his theory. Wegener earned support from a few colleagues, including Arthur Holmes (1890–

1965), who in 1929 demonstrated that thermal convection of the mantle might be responsible for moving the continents. Tragically, Wegener froze to death in 1930 while crossing the Greenland ice cap during one of his expeditions. He never witnessed the widespread acceptance that his theory would eventually earn as the nature of tectonic plates became clearer, and the role of mid-oceanic ridges on plate movements was understood. Wegener's theory was certainly

The last photo of Alfred Wegener (left) and Rasmus Villumsen, taken on November 1, 1930, (Wegener's 50th birthday) while on a polar expedition.

not "of the footloose type," as his critics had once contended. Instead, Wegener's insightful ideas suggested an underlying mechanism explaining many key principles that affect life on the planet.

Although not applauded during his lifetime for his theory of continental drift, Wegener was given much-deserved credit for establishing a multidisciplinary approach to studying Earth science that influenced the rise of geophysics. Trained as an astronomer but focusing his career on meteorology and climatology, Wegener felt strongly that geology had to embrace other sciences to solve some of its biggest puzzles. Wegener made this clear in *The Origin of Continents and Oceans* when he wrote, "It is only by combing the information furnished by all the Earth sciences that we can hope to determine 'truth' here, that is to say, to find the picture that sets out all the known facts in the best arrangement and that therefore has the highest degree of probability."

Continental drift has caused dramatic changes to the size, shape, and location of continents. During the **Cambrian Period,** 550 million years ago, the continents consisted of many fragmented landmasses spread across the equator. The predominant organisms of that time included ocean life such as fish and **arthropods**.

By the time of the Middle Triassic Epoch, about 240 million years ago, the world's individual landmasses had clumped together to form the massive super continent that Wegener called Pangaea. Many forms of animal life populated land by that time, including amphibians, reptiles, primitive mammals, and the first dinosaurs.

The supercontinent Pangaea began to break apart about 200 million years ago. The breakup accelerated during the reign of the dinosaurs, which is why fossils of dinosaurs have now been found on every continent, including Antarctica. The continents approached their current configuration during the age of mammals, about 45 million years ago.

The continents are still on the move. Ever so gradually, Australia is making the most noticeable shift. The land of koalas is on a slow collision course with Asia, the land of pandas. This close encounter of these two continents will not happen, however, for many millions of years.

Stages of Continental Drift

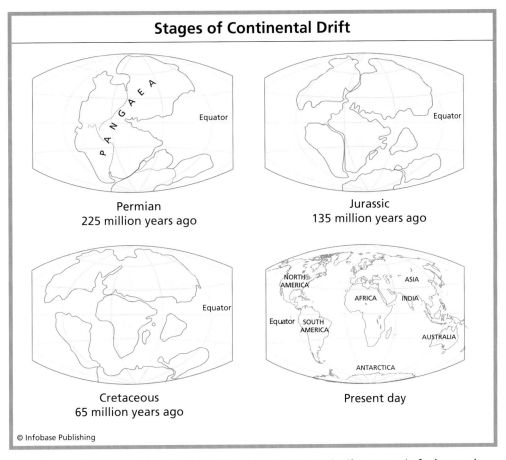

Permian
225 million years ago

Jurassic
135 million years ago

Cretaceous
65 million years ago

Present day

© Infobase Publishing

The stages of continental drift from 225 million years ago to the present. A slow and continuous process, continental drift has transformed the land mass Pangaea into separate continents.

How Continental Drift Affects Life

Continental drift affects more than the configuration of landmasses. It profoundly influences the direction that life can take. The movement of tectonic plates is a slow process by human time standards, but it modifies the entire **ecosystem** of a landmass, not only changing its geological features, but also affecting weather and organisms that inhabit the environment. The history of life is intimately linked to the history of the drifting continents.

Weather and climate are modified by shifts in landmasses for many reasons. When tectonic plates shift, they do not move about freely like rafts on a lake. They struggle with other bodies below them and around them, colliding, uplifting, and cleaving to form new mountains, plains, gullies, rivers, lakes, and other features. Such implacable geologic features may obviously create physical barriers to life that did not exist before, shrinking the geographic range of a species or making it more difficult for species to migrate and mingle. But each of these geologic shifts can also change patterns of wind, precipitation, and temperature. Land that was once at sea level might eventually rise several thousand feet, creating a cooler, more rugged environment. Animal species that once lived there would have to escape, adapt, or perish.

Weather on the continents is also subject to conditions that exist over the oceans. Ocean currents and circulation change largely because of heat from the Sun. Wind and precipitation over land are, in turn, affected by the temperature of the ocean and the direction of water currents. When continents shift, they affect the depth and surface area of the oceans. This not only alters the habitat of organisms that live in the ocean, but also modifies the climate on land, forcing species in both habitats to adapt as best they can.

Changes to local geology and climate are sufficiently challenging to revise the future of many species. But continental drift provokes yet another biological story. Each drifting continent is like a life boat for its inhabitants. These organisms become cut off from their ancestral stock. They become geographically isolated. This isolation changes the adaptive choices of a species and can sometimes be disastrous. When Antarctica drifted to its southerly location on the planet, and its climate took a change for the deep freeze, many kinds of animals and plants that once prospered there became extinct. They were replaced by organisms that could thrive in the subpolar icebox, including animals, such as penguins and seals, and plants, such as mosses and lichens.

The effect of being isolated on a continent does not always lead to disaster and less diversity, however. When the ability to roam over a larger geographic area is taken away, some species begin to develop and diversify in remarkable ways, discarding traits that might dominate the ancestors left behind on other continents. Geographic isolation leads to greater diversity of species because both groups that have been separated will continue to evolve in their own unique directions.

Fossil evidence makes it possible to see what happens to similar animals if they are suddenly and irrevocably separated by continental drift. There is no better case than the history of early mammals. Mammals first appeared about 200 million years ago when the continents were still relatively joined as Pangaea. These animals were small and resembled mice, rats, and squirrels. As the super continent began to break up, it formed two large landmasses in the Northern Hemisphere from which North America and Eurasia would emerge. In the Southern Hemisphere, a landmass called *Gondwana* included the pieces that would later make up South America, Africa, India, Australia, and Antarctica. As these landmasses divided and drifted apart, each took with it members of the early mammal species that had begun to thrive on Pangaea.

Australia and Antarctica were still joined when they jettisoned themselves from Gondwana about 100 million years ago. By about 65 million years ago, Australia and Antarctica parted ways and began to approach their present locations. The climate of the planet at that time, even in Antarctica, was mild and temperate, and mammals apparently loved it. Being separated from their ancestors in North America, Europe, South America, Asia, and Africa, however, led some separated mammals to a surprising turn.

Mammals are divided into two major groups; those that lay eggs and those that bear live young. Egg-bearing mammals are rare and consist of only a few species, including the duck-billed platypus. Mammals that bear live young are the predominant form and are further divided into three groups, the first of which is the pantotheres and includes only extinct forms. The two remaining groups still exist and include the marsupials, or pouched mammals, and the eutherians, or placental mammals. The vast majority of living mammals are eutherians, and they live on every continent. The marsupials are much rarer. A small number of marsupial species are still native to North America, but in Australia, marsupials remain a populous and vital part of the mammalian **fauna**, or animal life. This phenomenon can be attributed to continental drift.

After Pangaea divided, species of mammals were isolated on the different continents and developed as best they could. The seed for marsupials may have been planted before this split, and it appears that the first marsupials appeared in North and South America. Whereas eutherian mammals came to dominate the rise of mammals on other continents, the tables were turned in Australia. In no place are marsupials so prevalent as in Australia.

The prehistoric marsupials of Australia came in all sizes and often resembled nonmarsupial mammals from other continents, like hyenas, mice, moles, rats, and squirrels. Australia had a cat-sized marsupial "lion" (*Priscileo*), meat-eating kangaroos (*Ekaltadeta*), and cow-sized plant-eaters (*Neohelos*). The explosion of new marsupial species in Australia was made possible by continental drift and the geographic isolation of these mammals. Movement of the continent probably also explains why marsupials have continued to thrive in Australia today, whereas most marsupial species on other continents have disappeared. Once isolated, the continent of Australia continued to drift rapidly by geologic standards. Its climate changed from being mild and temperate to being tropical and scorching. Many of the marsupial species of Australia managed to adapt to this change, and their longevity, even in the wake of competition from eutherian mammals, can be attributed to their sturdy genetic stock.

GEOLOGY AND DEEP TIME

The science of geology represents a remarkable breakthrough in modern thought as important as the study of the atom, the understanding of gravity, and the exploration of outer space.

One of geology's major contributions to human knowledge is the measurement of the age of the Earth. The first modern geologists used everyday observation to demonstrate that the history of the Earth was much older than the history of humans. In fact, the planet is so old that its antiquity is difficult to explain in terms that most people can understand. Yet the study of prehistoric life requires a way to explain the age of the Earth and the physical conditions leading to the development of organisms. To get a grip on prehistory, scientists must be able to measure deep time, a scale of timekeeping embracing thousands, millions, and even billions of years.

The next chapter explains how geologists arrived at a system for measuring prehistoric time and ways that it is used to identify the sequence of geologic and biologic events that shaped the planet's past.

SUMMARY

This chapter introduced the composition of the Earth and the physical forces that account for its constantly changing structure.

1. Earth is 4.5 billion years old. The first forms of life arose about 3.5 billion years ago.
2. The Earth is made up of an inner core, an outer liquid core, a mantle, and a crust.
3. The surface of the Earth may seem stable and solid, but it is actually changing all the time.
4. Heat and gravity are the two main forces leading to all of the changes in Earth's surface.
5. Earth's surface is made up of many large slabs of crust called tectonic plates that ride on top of Earth's semiliquid and molten hot mantle. There are a dozen or more tectonic plates that interlock to make up the fragmented crust of the Earth.
6. Dry land—the continents—change their size and location due to the action of plate tectonics.
7. Widespread changes in Earth's geology significantly alter the survival and development of organisms.

2

GEOLOGIC TIME

The age of the Earth is an immense span of time. The first signs of life in the fossil record are also vastly distant. Understanding the origins and development of prehistoric life requires a suspension of everyday concepts about passing time.

Faced with the challenge of describing such long spans of time, geologists have developed a scale of measurement based on the geologic forces of the planet. This chapter explores how scientists arrived at this scale of measurement and how it is applied to the study of prehistoric life. The methods and tools geologists use to measure time provide the means for dating the remains of prehistoric organisms and assigning them to a timescale that is recognized the world over.

HOW OLD IS OLD?

To a child less than 10 years old, the Civil War in the United States seems like ancient history. Yet Abraham Lincoln delivered the Gettysburg Address to people who lived only six generations ago. William Shakespeare wrote *Hamlet* in England for a Globe Theater audience who lived only 16 generations ago. The ancient Egyptians made up one of the earliest civilizations, but even they were drawing hieroglyphics a mere 80 generations ago in the history of human kind.

A number in the range of 80 generations is still easy to comprehend. This is because the timescale of human history is based on units of time that normal people can experience. Human history is measured in seconds, minutes, days, weeks, months, years, decades, generations, and centuries. This timescale is more difficult to grasp, however, when applied to prehistoric times. The human species, *Homo sapiens*, first appeared about 300,000 years ago. That is equal to about 12,000 successive generations of human beings, a figure that stretches the useful limits of the human scale of experiencing time.

There can be more than one scale for measuring time, the human timescale being one of them. The scale by which time is measured depends largely on what is being measured. About two hundred years ago, scientists first began to understand that many forms of life existed before people, and they puzzled greatly over exactly how long ago this was. The very concept of **extinction**—that no species lasts forever—was a new idea in the nineteenth century. The concept of extinction meant that life was somehow imperfect, that species came and went, and that one day people, as a species, might also perish from the Earth. Fossils of ancient creatures provided scientists with proof that species became extinct. The same fossils also told scientists that many forms of life had come and gone over a long period of time before humans.

Prehistoric time is difficult to measure using the human timescale. Measuring prehistoric time requires a scale of measurement that goes back much further in time than the history of humans. Where is this timescale found? In the very rocks of the Earth itself.

Paleontologists turn to the geology of the Earth for a scale to measure prehistoric time. Early geologists working in the nineteenth century observed that rocks accumulated in layers, with the oldest on the bottom. The telltale signs of passing time have been recorded in the layers of rocks that make up the crust of the planet.

James Hutton, whose Plutonist theory was one of the first to explain the interior composition of the Earth, originated his theories about geological processes in the observation of natural forces that could be seen in the planet's crust. This principle, originating with Hutton, has been called **uniformitarianism**. Hutton proposed a natural cycle by which the Earth replenishes itself. Hutton theorized that rocks eroded from mountains were transported by rivers and streams to the ocean. In the ocean, these rocks sank as deposits to the bottom of the sea, where subterranean forces of heat and gravitational pressure turned them into rocks once again. The action of earthquakes and volcanoes might one day raise these newly formed rocks to the surface again, gradually forming new mountains and other land forms. The most startling aspect of Hutton's theory was that the time needed to accommodate this cycle was enormously long; much longer than human history or any timescale in use in the eighteenth century. Hutton intentionally gave no precise estimate of the age of the Earth, stating that it was probably infinitely old. He infuriated Abraham Gottlob Werner and his other critics with his intentionally vague and now famous statement that, "The result, therefore, of our present enquiry is, that we find no vestige of a beginning—no prospect of an end."

Hutton published his innovative ideas in the book *Theory of the Earth* (1785). Hutton is called the father of geology by many historians and can be credited with laying the foundation for modern geology. Because his writing was overly prosaic, however, and difficult to grasp, Hutton's radical ideas did not have much influence beyond a small inner circle of well-informed natural scientists.

Around the time of Hutton's death in 1797, a young British surveyor and mapmaker named William Smith (1769–1839) was making his own observations about rock strata on the British Isles. Working as a mining engineer, Smith observed that the rock strata into which mine shafts had been drilled contained a regular and predictable pattern of stratigraphic rock layers. These strata could be observed in widespread locations, suggesting a regularity to geologic formations. Furthermore, certain strata contained the same fossils, no matter where an outcropping of a given layer may lay. Smith was not a man of science, but his detailed stratigraphic maps of the area surrounding Bath (1799) and all of England (1815) were the first credible geologic maps.

The unsung work of Smith was echoed in France by the work geologist Gérard Paul Deshayes (1795–1875). Deshayes was an expert on fossil shells, and he obsessively cataloged nearly 3,000 individual species of extinct invertebrates and their associated rock strata around his native France. Like Hutton and Smith, Deshayes came to the conclusion that stratigraphic layers of rock had been laid down over long periods of time through natural forces that could be observed every day. By 1829, when Deshayes published his findings, he had become acquainted with the man who would successfully usher in the age of modern geologic study, Sir Charles Lyell (1797–1875).

Lyell, a British naturalist, was born the same year that James Hutton died. As if picking up where Hutton left off, Lyell's own fascination with Earth science was fueled by Hutton's innovative theories. The job of introducing Hutton's ideas to a wider audience became Lyell's passion. He traveled widely in search of evidence to prove that Hutton was correct and armed himself with compelling findings from colleagues such as Deshayes. Perhaps most importantly, Lyell was geology's first great communicator.

Lyell embraced Hutton's theory of uniformitarianism. In 1830, Lyell distilled this complex theory down to a simple guiding principle to explain the age of the Earth: The present is the key to the past. His momentous book *Principles of Geology* became the bible of geology and was revised 12 times in Lyell's lifetime.

Lyell's seemingly common-sense proposition—that observing the present is the key to understanding how geologic features were created over time—was a bold realization in his day. Prior to Lyell's thoughtful premise, it was generally accepted that God had created all life during the six days of biblical creation. Christian scholars had even used genealogies found in the Bible to calculate that the creation had taken place approximately 6,000 years ago. Lyell showed that past geological events were shaped by the same forces at work today. Given enough time to work, natural forces slowly and dramatically change the face of the Earth. These actions might take thousands, perhaps millions of years. Such an idea seemed impossible to those who believed that the Earth was only 6,000 years old. But soon many natural scientists and geologists began to back up the principle of uniformitarianism through the proof of observation.

From the work of early geologists came two basic guidelines for examining layers of the Earth; the principles of **superposition** and **cross-cutting**. Rock that forms in layers from the debris of other rocks or the remains of organisms is called sedimentary rock. The principle of superposition states that younger sedimentary rocks are deposited on top of older sedimentary rocks. The principle of cross-cutting states that any geologic feature is younger than anything else that it cuts across.

The time it takes today for layers of the Earth to accumulate through erosion, water transport, drought, and other forces, is the same time that it took in the past. This is an exceedingly slow process by human time standards, but it accounts for the ancient age of the Earth.

Communicating the length of time needed to explain the process of Earth's geologic features required geologists to develop a new scale for measuring time. The result was a timescale based on the layers of the Earth and how long these layers took to accumulate. This is called the **geologic time scale**. The development of this scale began with the work of William Smith, who created the first stratigraphic map. The layers were identified over time by examining their fossil contents and the positions of the layers in relation to one another. Because no given species of plant or animal exists forever, its fossil remains are restricted to certain layers. By studying and comparing layers of rock in different locations, geologists could see that the same layers were often in place, sometimes in areas of the world that were widely separated.

Smith's inaugural work in documenting stratigraphic layers was soon expanded to many other countries as geologists the world over took up the cause. Many of the names originally given to the Earth's stratigraphic layers by Smith and his immediate successors are still used today. The age of these stratigraphic layers was set down and revised continually by Sir Charles Lyell until his death in 1875.

By the end of the nineteenth century, there was widespread agreement that the Earth was many millions of years old. Just how many millions of years was still a matter of scientific debate. By 1860, the prevailing view, supported by Sir Charles Lyell, was that the Earth was a minimum of 200 million years old and perhaps as old as 340 million years. British physicist Lord Kelvin (1824–1907) strongly disagreed with this estimate, however, and waged a war of scientific inquiry using mathematical calculations rather than geologic observations of the Earth. Chief among his reasons were estimates of the time needed for Earth's interior to have cooled from a once-molten state, which is how he thought the planet had begun. Even though he was incorrect about a molten origin of the Earth—it was later shown that it had formed through an accumulation of smaller particles—Kelvin's stature in science and his indefatigable logic seemed beyond reproach. His estimate of the age of the Earth was between 20 million and 40 million years old, a view that prevailed for about 40 years.

What overthrew Kelvin's estimate was the discovery, in 1895, of radioactivity. An understanding of radioactive isotopes and the rate at which they decay over many millions of years made it possible to date many layers of the Earth, with little doubt, to within years.

The current calculation that the Earth is 4.5 billion years old was arrived at around 1953. Although there are continuing refinements of the ages of individual strata within the geologic timescale, these changes are usually small, only affecting minor adjustments to the beginnings and ends of previously identified time spans.

RELATIVE DATING

Through the widespread study of exposed rock layers all over the world, geologists have been able to visualize and record an ideal "geologic column" representing all possible layers from the earliest rock layers to the present. Of course, there is no single place on Earth where all of these layers can be observed at one time. Earth's crust is too fragmented and twisted for that. But it is clear that a uniform set of natural forces has shaped the crust of the Earth over an immense ocean of time. Determining the date of one layer of the Earth by comparing it to one of the previously identified layers is called **relative dating**.

Just how old are the layers of rock? By calculating the time it took for the many layers of the Earth to build up over time, the immensity of geologic time quickly becomes apparent. Whereas a timescale based on human experience deals in tens and hundreds of years, the geologic timescale works in millions and billions of years. To make these staggering chunks of time easier to understand, the geologic timescale is broken down into time intervals of decreasing size:

Eon. The longest spans of time in Earth's history are divided into three **eons.** The first eon, called the Archean ("ancient"), ranged from the earliest Earth to about 2.5 billion years ago. This was the time of Earth's earliest development and was mostly devoid of life. The second eon, the Proterozoic ("early life"), began after the Archean Eon and lasted until about 542 million years ago. During this stage, the climate and geology of the Earth settled down enough for the development of the first complex life-forms. The first multicelled animals and invertebrates have roots in the Proterozoic Eon. The third eon, called the Phanerozoic ("visible life"), began 542 million years ago and is the present eon. The Phanerozoic Eon is marked by the widespread **evolution** and distribution of life across the planet. Evolution is the natural process that causes species to change gradually over time. This is the eon from which most fossil evidence for past life comes, and which will be the subject of this book.

Era. The Archean Eon is divided into four **eras** dating from 2.5 billion to more than 4 billion years ago. This was the time of the formation and stabilizing of the planet Earth and the emergence of the earliest, single-celled life-forms about 3.5 billion years ago. The Proterozoic Eon is divided into three eras dating from about 542 million years ago to 2.5 billion years ago. The earliest forms of multicelled organisms first appeared during the end of this eon. The Phanerozoic Eon is divided into three eras: the Paleozoic, Mesozoic, and Cenozoic. The Paleozoic ("ancient life") Era lasted from 542 million to 251 million years ago and was noted for the appearance of early invertebrates, fishes, land plants, amphibians, and reptiles. The Mesozoic ("middle life") Era lasted from 251 million to 65 million years ago and was noted for the rise of the dinosaurs, marine reptiles, flying reptiles, and birds. The Cenozoic ("recent life") Era began 65 million years ago and continues to the present. The Cenozoic Era has been marked by the rise of the mammals and the emergence of humans.

Period. **Periods** are subdivisions of eras and are the time intervals that are used most frequently in this book to refer to specific kinds of prehistoric life. The Phanerozoic Eon is divided into three eras and 11 periods, each of which covers a span of millions of years. The longest of these periods, including the three in the Mesozoic Era, are sometimes further broken down. The Triassic Period, for example, is divided into Early, Middle, and Late epochs, referring to their relative age in the layers of the Earth. The Early Triassic Epoch is older (that is, found underneath) the Middle Triassic Epoch. Some of these epochs are based on sedimentary rock sequences, fossils, and even absolute time. In this book, however, the period is the smallest time interval that will normally be identified.

The lengths of eons, eras, periods, and epochs were not arrived at arbitrarily. All periods, for example, are not of equal length. While to make them of equal length may have made them easier to understand, to base them arbitrarily on time divisions of equal length would have betrayed the nature of the geologic timescale. The lengths of eons, eras, and periods are not arbitrary at all, but are based on the geology of the Earth layers that mark their beginnings and ends. Some of these layers took longer than others to accumulate, which accounts for the different lengths of these ancient time intervals. Many of the major divisions between geologic time spans are also marked by significant geologic events, such as mass extinctions, glaciations, and widespread volcanic activity.

ABSOLUTE DATING

Relative dating using clues from Earth's layers provides an approximate time during which an organism lived. This form of dating uses evidence found in sedimentary rocks. To say, however, that an animal lived in the Cretaceous Period (which was 80 million years long), or even in the Upper Cretaceous Period (which lasted for 34 million years), leaves many millions of years' variance.

A more precise method of dating rocks and fossils was developed during the latter half of the twentieth century. Called **absolute dating,** or radiometric dating, it can specify the age of a fossil within a range of years that is more geologically precise than relative dating.

Absolute dating was born with the study of radioactive elements during the early twentieth century. It was discovered that some naturally occurring elements—such as uranium, potassium, and carbon—can have unstable nuclei that break down over time. Such elements are said to be radioactive. As the nuclei of these atoms break down, the atoms gradually change to become atoms of another element. Radioactive uranium, for example, slowly changes into lead over time. Radioactive potassium slowly changes into argon, and radioactive carbon transforms into nitrogen. These changes are slow but occur at a constant rate. Scientists know exactly how long it takes for a given amount of one radioactive element to transform into another element. The age of a rock containing a radioactive element can therefore be determined by measuring the amounts of the radioactive element and the resulting element into which it is changing.

Of the radioactive elements just mentioned, only carbon can be found in the remains, or fossils, of living organisms. Radioactive uranium and potassium are found in igneous rocks that were formed under extremely high temperatures, including volcanic rock and ash.

If the remains of a living organism are less than 50,000 years old, they can sometimes be dated by analyzing radiometric traces of the element carbon. **Carbon-14 dating** is based on a simple principle associated with living organisms. Plants and animals absorb the element carbon throughout their lives. The process begins with plants that take in ordinary carbon from carbon dioxide in the air. Animals absorb carbon by eating plants or by eating animals that ate plants. These same organisms also take in another form of carbon—carbon 14—from the atmosphere. As long as an organism is alive, the proportion of ordinary carbon to carbon 14 in its system remains constant. When the animal or plant dies, however, it no longer absorbs carbon 14, and the amount left behind begins to decay at a constant rate, eventually changing into nitrogen. Scientists know the proportion of ordinary carbon to carbon 14 that should be present in a living thing, making it possible to calculate approximately how long ago the organism died. Carbon-14 dating is limited, however, to organisms that lived up to about 50,000 years ago. Longer ago than that, there is not enough carbon 14 left to measure with any accuracy.

Absolute dating involving radioactive uranium or potassium does not work directly on fossils, but on rocks found in the sedimentary deposits surrounding the fossils, such as the remains of an ancient flow of lava or ash. Radiometric dating can also be used to date layers of sediment directly above and below the layer in which a fossil is found. Volcanic ash is particularly good for making a radiometric dating using the potassium-argon method. If fossil remains are found between two layers of volcanic ash—which is likely in some, but not most fossil sites—the fossils can be dated to a point in time between the two layers of ash. Because of its rate of radioactive decay, potassium-argon dating is best used on samples that are 100,000 years old or more. Uranium-lead dating can be used to approximate times that can be measured in millions and billions of years.

GEOLOGIC TIME AND LIFE OF THE PAST

The concept of geologic time is a key to understanding prehistoric life. The geologic timescale is based on the length of time layers within Earth's crust have accumulated through the natural forces

THINK ABOUT IT

How Old Is Life? A Tape Measure of Life on Earth

It is difficult to imagine the stunningly long span of time that life has existed on Earth. This exercise will help you get a grip on the scope of prehistoric time.

Using a scale of 10,000,000 (10 million) years to every inch, you can create a tape measure of life on Earth. Begin with a 27-foot (8 m) length of ribbon or paper adding-machine tape. The start of the ribbon marks the present day. Mark off each foot or meter. Using a ruler and the following chart as a guide, mark off significant events in the development of life on Earth. The entire span of life as known from the fossil record is about 3.5 billion years.

The astounding realization revealed by this tape measure of time is that, although life has existed in one form or another for over 26 feet (7.9 m) of the tape measure, modern humans have been around only for the equivalent of one-quarter of an inch (0.6 cm) of this time.

TAPE MEASURE OF LIFE ON EARTH

Life-form	Approximate Number of Years Ago	Distance on Tape Measure from Present (in Feet/ Inches; Meters or Centimeters)
First fossil organisms	3,200,000,000	26' 7" (8 m)
First shellfish and corals	550,000,000	4' 6" (1.4 m)
First fishes	515,000,000	4' 4" (1.3 m)
First land plants	443,000,000	3' 8" (1.1 m)
First amphibians	365,000,000	3' 1" (0.9 m)
First reptiles	300,000,000	2' 6" (0.8 m)
First dinosaurs	225,000,000	1' 10" (0.6 m)
First mammals	210,000,000	1' 9" (0.5 m)
First birds	145,000,000	1' 3" (0.4 m)
First flowering plants	125,000,000	1' 0" (0.3 m)
First horses	50,000,000	0' 5" (12.7 cm)
First monkeys	40,000,000	0' 4" (10.2 cm)
First apes	30,000,000	0' 3" (07.6 cm)
First hominids	5,000,000	0' 0.5" (01.27 cm)
First modern humans	300,000	0' 0.025" (0.6 cm)

of erosion and deposition. Many of these sedimentary layers also contain the remains of extinct organisms. These ancient remains, or fossils, are the best clues available to the kinds of plants and animals that once inhabited the Earth.

The next chapter will explore the study of fossils and what they can reveal about the physical, anatomical, and behavioral nature of extinct organisms.

SUMMARY

This chapter explored the methods and tools scientists use to measure time and date the remains of prehistoric organisms.

1. The human timescale is just one scheme for measuring time.
2. Geologists and paleontologists turn to the geology of the Earth for a scale to measure prehistoric time.
3. Rock that forms in layers from the debris of other rocks or the remains of organisms is called *sedimentary rock*.
4. The principle of superposition states that younger sedimentary rocks are deposited on top of older sedimentary rocks.
5. The principle of cross-cutting states that any geologic feature is younger than anything else that it cuts across.
6. The geologic timescale was developed by geologists to measure time based on the layers of Earth's crust and how long these layers took to accumulate.
7. Determining the date of one layer of the Earth by comparing it to one of the previously identified layers is called *relative dating*. Relative dating may only be accurate within a range of several million years.
8. The geologic timescale is broken down into time intervals of decreasing size: eons, eras, and periods.
9. Absolute dating specifies the age of a fossil within a range of years.

SECTION TWO:
How Prehistoric Life Is Revealed

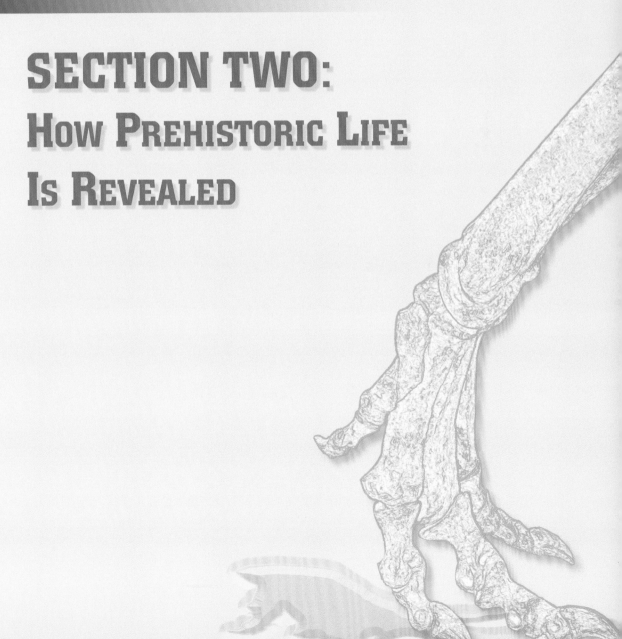

3

FOSSILS: CLUES TO PAST LIFE

Fossils are a window to prehistoric life. Paleontologists use fossils to form a view of the structure and lifestyles of extinct organisms. Organisms that become fossilized range from the smallest microorganisms to the largest animals on the planet, including those that live on land or in the sea. Without fossils, there would be few clues to the history of life before humans.

The making of a fossil is a rare event. The worldwide record of fossil creatures represents just a small fraction of the many millions of species that have ever existed. Even so, without fossils, there would be little knowledge of the kinds of organisms that existed in the past.

This chapter describes the types of fossils and how they are made. The environmental and geologic circumstances that make fossils possible are explored, as are as the remarkable kinds of information that fossils reveal about past life.

FOSSILS DEFINED

Fossils are the paleontologist's key to understanding prehistoric life. The word *fossil* means "something dug up" in Latin. A fossil is the trace of any organism—plant or animal—that has been preserved in the layers of the Earth.

Fossils have fascinated people for as long as there have been people. Trinkets found among the 35,000-year-old remains of Neandertals at Saint Léon, France, included a fossil brachiopod shell dating from the Jurassic Period. The ancient Greeks documented a variety of fossils and speculated on their origin. One of the earliest such observations to come down to us was written by the Greek historian

58

and explorer Herodotus (484 B.C.–ca. 425 B.C.). While traveling in northern Africa around 2,450 years ago, he found fossil seashells in the desert. Herodotus correctly speculated that the Mediterranean Sea had once flowed deep where deserts now lay.

HOW FOSSILS ARE FORMED

The making of a fossil is a rare event. The chance of winning a state lottery, with odds averaging 7 million to 1, is a "sure thing" compared to the chance that an organism will become a fossil. **Fossilization** is so unusual that only a tiny fraction of past life has been fossilized. Only about one-tenth of 1 percent of all species of prehistoric animals is known from fossils. This is even more remarkable when one takes into account that most species are represented by hundreds of thousands or even millions of individuals.

To become a fossil, an organism must die and then be buried quickly by sediment such as sand, mud, or volcanic ash. Being buried is essential so that the body is not completely eaten by other animals and does not have a chance to quickly rot away. Most animals that die do not get buried, but it is possible for burial to happen in several ways. If an animal dies and falls into a stream, its body can lie stationary and undisturbed while currents gradually cover it with sediment. A spectacular example of such stream burial was discovered in the badlands of western Canada in 1977. In this case, a bone bed containing the jumbled skeletons of up to 400 horned dinosaurs, young and old, provides evidence that part of a great herd of animals perished while trying to cross a flood-swollen river some 75 million years ago. Their remains were washed downstream and accumulated in a crook in the riverbed, where the dinosaurs became fossilized.

Animals may also be buried alive. Some 25,000 years ago, prehistoric mammals wandered unwittingly into the natural liquid asphalt pits found in what today is Rancho La Brea, California. The animals sank into the ooze, which later became hardened and preserved their bodies. Another unusually large death assemblage occurred in what is now Montana, about 75 million years ago. An area populated by as many as 10,000 *Maiasaura*, duck-billed dinosaurs, was suddenly overcome by poisonous volcanic gas and buried in ash. This event was so sudden and deadly that the dinosaurs were stopped in their tracks. Many examples of *Maiasaura* egg nests from this location include the fossils of baby and juvenile dinosaurs that perished while sitting in their nests.

Once buried, the body of an organism can remain undisturbed for long periods of time, even millions of years. The hardest parts of the body, such as bones and teeth, are protected by being buried. The soft tissues, including the skin, organs, and muscles, quickly dry up, rot away, and are eaten by bacteria and other microorganisms. As time goes on, sedimentary layers continue to build up on top of the creature's resting place, further protecting the remains from airborne bacteria. The layers that build up on top of the buried organism become heavier and heavier. Sometimes, these layers exert great pressure on the remains, flattening out the bones. At other times, however, the bones may not be flattened or distorted at all. Water and the minerals it carries seep into the sediment in which the bones are buried. At this point, the organism buried in the rock is well along the way to becoming a fossil.

Sometimes, the local climate may change sharply over a long period of time. What was once a lush tropical forest when an organism was buried may turn hot and dry. A case in point is that of the badlands of present-day Alberta, Canada. When dinosaurs roamed this region 75 million years ago, the climate was moist and tropical, more like present-day Miami, Florida. It was a lush, humid habitat alive with crocodiles, turtles, tropical greenery, and warm waterways. World climate gradually changes over time, however, which is often good for fossilization. When the formerly moist and pliable sediment that buried an organism becomes a layer of rock, its body fossil is solidly entombed for posterity.

Although some body parts, including teeth, may occasionally be preserved without undergoing a chemical change, most body fossils are transformed from purely organic material such as bones, blood, tissue, and organs to a combination of bone and stone. The process that causes this change is called **mineralization**. Water seeping through the laycr of carth that contains the bones brings with it minerals from the surrounding layers. These minerals often include silica, calcite, and iron. While much of the original bone material remains in place, many microscopic spaces in the bone can be filled up with the tiny particles of minerals that seep down through the ground. This eventually results in a bone that consists partly of original organic material and partly of minerals from the ground. The bone may then become quite heavy and have the sheen of stone.

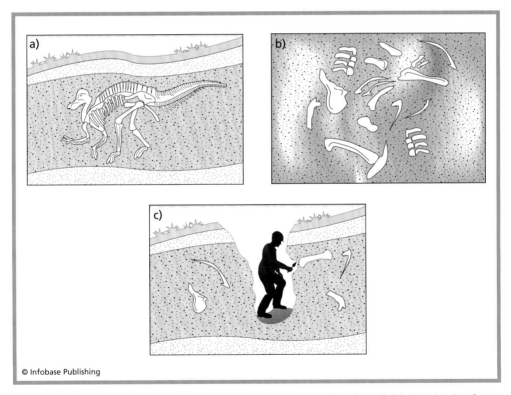

© Infobase Publishing

How a fossil could have formed: An animal died on a mud bank or fell into a body of water. The body rotted, sank, and was scavenged, leaving only bones (a). Mud or sand covered the bones, preventing further decay or scavenging, and allowed mineralization to take place (b). Over time, additional layers of sediment covered the specimen. Eventually erosion, uplift of the soil, or human activity removed the sedimentary layers covering the specimen, revealing it as a fossil (c).

The process of mineralization takes at least 10,000 years. Bones that are younger than that show little signs of mineralization, if any.

Most fossils consist of only part of an organism. There are many reasons for this. The carcass of an animal may have been scavenged before it was buried. An exposed part could have dried up and disintegrated in the heat of the Sun. If a creature died in a stream or river, its body could have broken apart, leaving only a part of it to get buried in sediment. Many fossil skeletons of large dinosaurs, such as the long-necked sauropods *Apatosaurus*, are incomplete because their huge bodies were probably only partially buried. Many sauropods are also found without heads. The reason for this is that the heavy head of the rotting dinosaur probably broke off its slender neck and so was separated from the body.

As mentioned earlier, the majority of fossils that exist in the Earth's crust will never see the light of day. They will remain buried deep in the layers of the Earth, never to be discovered by curious humans. Fortunately for paleontologists, however, Earth's crust is in motion. The massive forces of heat and gravity that move tectonic plates sometimes thrust upward, exposing a layer to the forces of weather and erosion. Given enough time, a fossil once buried deep within the crust may become exposed to the light of day for a lucky person to discover.

TYPES OF FOSSILS

By definition, a fossil is any trace of an organism preserved in the layers of Earth. The most familiar fossils are the bones of extinct creatures. Fossil skeletons, shells, teeth, and other hard body parts are preserved by the process of mineralization. There are, however, several other kinds of fossils produced by other natural processes.

An exhibit in a natural history museum showcases many kinds of fossils. The most spectacular are body fossils or skeletons, mounted in eye-catching exhibits, defying the ages so that people may experience the size and shape of long-lost creatures of Earth. In addition to fossil skeletons, a museum might display several other kinds of equally fascinating clues to past life. There might be footprints of dinosaurs, preserved in rock. There might be a rock showing an impression of skin, feathers, or hair from an extinct creature. Mounted on the wall might be the inky impression of an ancient sea creature or plant, preserved as a black silhouette that looks like a vivid painting. In the rarest of cases, a museum might display organic parts of an organism, preserved through a freakish accident of nature, that provide a glimpse at a relatively undisturbed carcass. These physical traces of prehistoric life are all types of fossils. They fall into the groups described below.

Body Fossils

The most common types of fossils are mineralized body parts such as bones, shells, and teeth. These are produced through the process of mineralization. The skeleton of a dinosaur, the skull of an early ape, and the shell of an extinct turtle are all examples of body fossils.

Molds and Casts

Sometimes the buried body parts of an organism completely dissolve away. This can happen when the ground water seeping through the fossil is acidic because of minerals in the surrounding earth. When the body part dissolves away, it leaves a hollow, or **mold,** of the original part. This happens frequently with fossil seashells, which are the bodies of extinct invertebrates. A mold can retain the finest detail of the shape and surface texture of the original body part. A mold fossil is similar to the impression that can be made by pressing one's fingertip into a piece of soft clay; close inspection reveals that the whorl of one's fingerprint is left in the mold.

If a mold is later filled with another mineral, a **cast** may be formed. A cast can retain the outer shape and size of the original body part in great detail.

Dinosaur skin is sometimes preserved in the form of a cast or mold. Although none of the original skin has been left behind, a mold or cast reveals the texture and size of the scales in remarkable detail.

A mold fossil of a prehistoric worm. Mold fossils can provide intricate details in the shape and texture of some extinct organisms.

Carbon Film Impressions

As the organic material is dissolved away by groundwater, it sometimes leaves behind a residue of carbon that forms a kind of shadow image or outline of the organism. Fossils of sea creatures, such as fishes and ichthyosaurs, are often found with mineralized bones and a carbon outline of their body.

Prehistoric plants are often preserved in the form of carbon film impressions. Although none of their original organic material remains, such finely detailed fossils can reveal much about plant life from the past, right down to its cellular structure.

Mummification

One of the rarest and most revealing forms of fossil preservation is the natural mummy. This occurs when an animal's carcass dries out in the hot sun, undisturbed by predators, before being buried by sand. Mummies can also form in the stable, dry environment of some caves. The skin and soft tissues of the animal desiccate, or dry out, and hug tightly to the bones. Once the carcass is buried, mineralization takes

A carbon film impression of a plantlike organism. Carbon impressions are formed when groundwater washes away organic material, leaving behind fossils like this.

place, leaving a fine impression of the skin and some of the soft tissues. The most famous fossil mummy is that of the duck-billed dinosaur *Edmontosaurus*. This specimen is displayed in the American Museum of Natural History in New York as it was originally found, lying on its back with one arm in the air, its head drawn back, and its knees bent. Much of the body is covered with the fossil impressions of skin, clearly showing the similarity of dinosaur skin to that of other reptiles.

Preservation in Amber

Amber is a substance formed from the hardened sap of ancient trees. Occasionally, fossils of insects, plants, and other small organisms are found preserved in amber. How did they get there? Tree sap is sticky stuff. A hapless insect landing on a drop of sap could have become trapped and unable to pry itself loose. Perhaps a small creature may have been covered by sap falling from a higher tree branch. In either case, it would be difficult to escape this gooey fate. Once the creature was totally covered, it would die and the sap would harden, preserving the creature's body trapped inside.

Most creatures fossilized in amber have dried away, leaving remarkably well-preserved outside shells of their bodies. This preservation leaves much to examine. A scientist using an electron microscope to get a close-up look at an insect trapped in amber can detect traces of an insect's flight muscles and cell fibers from their shells.

In the book and movie *Jurassic Park*, scientists extract traces of dinosaur **DNA** (genetic material) from blood-sucking insects

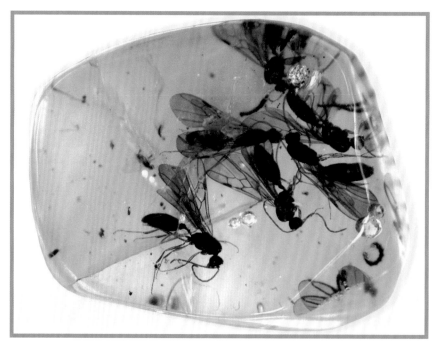

Amber, or hardened tree sap, can reveal fossils of insects, plants, or other small organisms that were trapped within it.

trapped in amber. Is this actually possible? A few scientists claim to have extracted bacteria and DNA from creatures trapped in amber, but follow-up studies by other scientists have not been able to reproduce their results. For the time being, the door seems to be closed on the possibility of finding DNA of any sort in amber, let alone DNA that is as old as the dinosaurs. Scientists cannot reliably recover DNA from fossils that are older than 50,000 years. Other experimenters have analyzed the air trapped in amber bubbles, concluding in some cases that the atmosphere during the Late Cretaceous Epoch was richer in oxygen than the atmosphere today.

Nature's Freezer Case

In 1900, a Russian hunter was tracking a wounded deer in the Beresovka River valley of Siberia. What he found instead sent many a scientific expedition scampering to the frozen arctic regions of Siberia. Staring out at the hunter from a wall of frozen soil was the partially uncovered head of an elephantlike creature. This discovery turned out to be the long-frozen carcass of a wooly mammoth, the kind of creature previously known mostly from fossil skeletons and cave drawings. In 1901, after four months of grueling travel across 3,000 miles (4,800 km) of the Siberian north, a team of Russian scientists arrived to excavate the beast. The expedition was led by zoologists Otto Herz and Eugen Pfizenmayer of the Russian Imperial Academy of Sciences. By the time they finally reached the site, part of the beast had melted out, leaving its flesh exposed to the elements. Nonetheless, it was a startling site to see the beast staring back at them. "We stood speechless in front of this evidence of the prehistoric world," wrote Pfizenmayer, "which had been preserved almost intact in its grave of ice throughout the ages." The internal organs of the beast had long since rotted away, but some of the frozen meat of its hindquarters and other outer layers appeared somewhat fresh. According to the account of the expedition, the flesh was "dark red in color and looked as fresh as well-frozen beef or horse meat." Some of the mammoth had been gnawed away by hungry predators. Members of the expedition even fed their dogs scraps of the meat. A close look at the circumstances surrounding the mammoth's fate revealed how it had perished. The animal had fallen with a landslide some 39,000 years ago, where it was mortally injured and died sitting up, just as it was found.

The frozen wooly mammoth, although tens of thousands of years old, was not subject to the kinds of physical changes that occur with other fossils. Instead of having parts that were mineralized, cast, or carbonized, the mammoth consisted entirely of its original flesh, blood, bones, and organs. The creature was somewhat freezer burned, but nonetheless original "grade A" choice wooly mammoth. Since then, more than 50 other frozen carcasses, mostly mammoths, have been found in Arctic regions from Siberia to Alaska. The oldest have been carbon-dated to between 11,000 and 40,000 years ago.

In 1991, the world took notice when hikers Erika and Helmut Simon stumbled upon the body of a man lying on the ground in the Austrian Alps. Carbon dating determined that the frozen carcass was about 5,300 years old, making it the oldest preserved remains of a human being ever discovered. Nicknamed Ötzi the Iceman, it is another example of a frozen, rather than mineralized, body that has come to light after many thousands of years. Examination of his body revealed that the Iceman had been mortally wounded by an arrow. His clothing and possessions were also splattered with the blood of at least four other people. It seems that Ötzi had been engaged in a pitched battle during which he was struck by an arrow. Even though he was hurt, he scampered off to a quiet place where he died. His remains included clothing and many artifacts that provide clues to his life, skills, and knowledge. Among his possessions were a bow, arrows, and quiver; an ax; a simple backpack made of wood and cords; two containers made of birchbark; a knife with a woven sheath; a belt pouch; a tassel with a stone bead; and a medicine bag containing several medicinal fungi.

Trace Fossils

All of the fossils discussed so far are types of body fossils. They preserve an actual part of the body of an organism or a fossil impression—that is, a mold or cast—of a body part. Another kind of fossil,

This trace fossil of a dinosaur footprint can provide evidence of past life through the impression captured in sedimentary rock.

called a **trace fossil,** reveals evidence of past life without preserving any body parts. Types of trace fossils include footprints, skin impressions, burrows, bite marks, egg nests, and even preserved dung.

WHAT FOSSILS TELL US

Fossil bones and body parts provide many clues to the **anatomy** of an organism. Anatomy consists of the basic biological systems of an animal, such as the skeletal and muscular systems. Although muscles themselves are soft tissue that does not fossilize, bones often show scars and wear marks where muscles were once attached. Bones and other body fossils show the size and shape of an individual animal at the time of its death. Bones can tell how long a dinosaur was, how tall a wooly mammoth stood, and whether an early member of the whale family could swim. If many specimens of the same kind of organism are found, it may be possible to understand how fast it grew, how the males and females of the species differed in shape and size, how old an individual may have been when it died, and how big a species could become.

Skeletal features are also a key to the **physiology** of an organism. Physiology is the study of such body functions as eating, running, fighting, mating, foraging, and other tasks needed to survive. Whereas anatomy shows how an animal was *put together,* physiology describes the way an animal's parts *worked together* and were adapted to help the organism survive.

Many of its body parts show how an animal was adapted to its world. The shape and organization of teeth reveal the diet of a creature. Other parts of the body, such as the backbone, tail, head, hands, and feet, help explain how an animal protected itself or may have hunted its prey.

Trace fossils do not reveal the size or shape of an organism but do reveal much about its behavior and even its physiology. Fossilized dinosaur dung, called **coprolite** by paleontologists, can contain traces of a dinosaur's meal. Although scientists cannot say for sure which kind of dinosaur left the fossil feces, they can see that it ate plants or animals or both. Sometimes, the droppings left by a plant-eating animal include such clear traces of its meal that it is possible to identify the kind of plant that it ate. This information helps to expand our understanding of the ecology of prehistoric time—the way in which plants and animals lived together in the environment.

Fossil footprints, also called **trackways,** reveal much about the track maker. As with coprolite, it is impossible to know for sure which kind of creature left a track. But when knowledge of trackways is combined with that of fossil bones found in the same location, it is possible to make a good guess as to the track maker. In the case of dinosaurs, meat-eating dinosaurs had three sharply clawed toes, whereas plant-eating dinosaurs had three to five toes with rounded or even blunt tips. Sometimes a trackway can show that a meat-eater might have been following its next meal. A trackway consisting of a trail left by many similar individuals provides evidence that the animals traveled in herds. Most astoundingly, it is possible to calculate the speed of a track maker when there is an uninterrupted series of tracks laid down by the same individual.

WHAT BECOMES FOSSILIZED?

Fossils are created by a series of chance events. When an animal dies, many possible things can happen to its body. In most cases, it will be scavenged by other animals, insects, and bacteria, thereby providing food for other organisms in the continuing cycle of life. What is left may weather under the hot sun or be washed away in pieces. Some pieces may be carried away by birds or insects. The skeleton may break apart and lie on a forest bed with falling leaves, becoming part of the mulch that nourishes the dirt so that other plants may grow. One of the most unlikely options is that the body will be left relatively undisturbed, buried by sediment, and sealed in rock, where its secrets may remain intact for millions of years.

Making a fossil clearly requires a lot of luck, but are there factors that make fossilization more likely for some organisms than others? The answer is yes. Paleontologists speak of **bias** in the fossil record to explain why some forms of prehistoric life are more likely than others to become fossils.

The word *bias* is often used to describe people who have a strong natural leaning toward one side of an argument. Similarly, when making fossils, nature has a strong leaning toward certain combinations of living conditions, types of organisms, and habitats.

Natural circumstances that favor fossilization can be separated into four groups: population, anatomy, size, and biology and habitat. All of these factors contribute significantly to the likelihood of a member of a species becoming a fossil.

Population. When playing the odds of fossilization, "the more the merrier" is an apt motto. If a species **population** is large, it is more likely that at least one member of that population will become a fossil. Compare this to going to a baseball game and looking through the stadium for a girl with green eyes—a less common trait found in humans. If the seeker picks only a single row of seats in one section of the stadium in which to find a girl with green eyes, it is less likely that such a girl will be found. The chances of finding a girl with green eyes improve immensely if the seeker considers the entire population of the stadium. There is no guarantee that a girl with green eyes will be in the stadium, but it is more likely when a larger population is present. Likewise, a large species population does not guarantee that some individuals will become fossilized, but the odds are increased.

Anatomy. The structure of an organism's body is one of the most important factors leading to fossilization. Large, hard body parts are more likely to be preserved than soft body parts. These large, hard parts include vertebrate bones, mollusk shells, tree trunks, the **exoskeletons** (outer skeletons) of arthropods, and other rigid body parts. The internal skeletons, or **endoskeletons**, of vertebrates are usually made of hard bone consisting of phosphate and calcium. Bones are ideal for fossilization. The bigger the bones, the better for fossilization. Finding a relatively complete fossil skeleton, however, is uncommon. In life, bones are held together by soft tissue such as muscles and tendons. After a creature dies, and these soft parts rot, the skeleton often falls apart and scatters.

Cartilage is another skeletal material. Unlike bone, it is soft and flexible, like gristle. The outer ear and nose of humans is made of cartilage. Sharks, dogfishes, and rays are the most familiar surviving members of an ancient class of cartilaginous fishes. Because their skeletal parts are rarely found in the fossil record, they are known mostly from teeth, scales, and some remarkable carbon film impressions showing the outline and soft tissues of the body. When it comes to leaving behind a body fossil, however, the odds heavily favor animals with bones over those with cartilage.

Size. Being a big creature increases the chance of becoming a fossil. Big bones are more likely to become fossils. Large bones, shells, body armor, and other hard body parts are stronger and less likely to be crumbled by nature's natural forces. Large fossils are also more likely to be discovered by a passing rock hound or paleontologist. For these reasons, the factor of size also introduces another kind of bias in the interpretation of the past; that of thinking that the ancient world was mostly populated by giant creatures. This is a distortion of past life because smaller creatures normally outnumber large ones. Finding large fossil animals only provides a partial view of prehistoric ecosystems. Realizing this, many paleontologists have returned to fossil sites made famous by the discovery of giant animals to look for traces of smaller creatures that may have passed unnoticed before.

Biology and habitat. The lifestyle of an organism greatly affects the chance that it may one day become a fossil. Because fossils are created by the burial of dead organisms in layers of sediment, living and dying near a watery environment increases an organism's chances of becoming a fossil. An animal or plant that dies in a shallow sea is more likely to become a fossil than an organism that dies in a dry, barren environment lacking rain. The habitat in which an organism dies must also be able to protect the body so that it can become a fossil. Some creatures die and become buried as a result of natural catastrophes such as volcanic eruptions, sandstorms, and floods. Any organism living in an environment prone to such disasters has a greater chance of becoming a fossil. Geological occurrences after an organism's death ultimately determine whether it

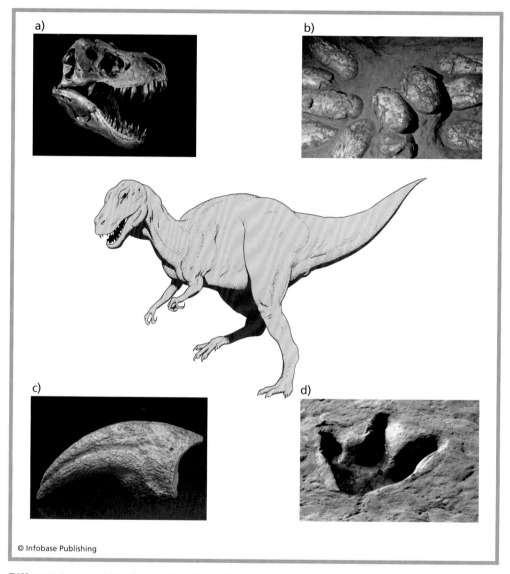

a)

b)

c)

d)

© Infobase Publishing

Different types of fossils may be found from one organism. The *Tyrannosaurus rex* in the center might yield fossils of its (a) skull, (b) eggs, (c) claw, or (d) footprints.

will become a fossil or will ever be discovered. Many fossils are buried deep in the crust and may never come to light. Only those that are exposed to the surface through erosion, the buckling of Earth's crust, or other natural events will ever be close enough to ground level for people to find them.

FINDING AND DATING FOSSILS

In the early years of the science of geology, during the first half of the nineteenth century, a tremendous effort was made to record and date exposures of Earth's crust. This effort began in Europe and spread around the globe. In the late nineteenth century, many geologists in the United States explored the frontiers of the West to document its geologic features. The United States Geological Survey (USGS) was founded for this purpose. Year after year, during the better part of the 1800s, geologists and paleontologists traveled widely across the country to document its mineral resources and stratigraphic layers. Many significant fossil deposits of North America were discovered because of these government-funded surveys. These efforts also were important for discoveries of natural mineral resources such as iron ore, coal, and other materials. The scientists of the USGS also helped map a geologic history of North America that could be compared to those of Europe, Asia, and other continents. Chief among the leading paleontologists of the United States who took part in these surveys were Joseph Leidy (1823–1891), Othniel Charles Marsh (1831–1899), Edward Drinker Cope (1840–1897), and Henry Fairfield Osborn (1857–1935).

Finding fossils is not as easy as going into your backyard with a shovel and starting to dig. Although this might work in some places, the chances are not great that you just happen to live on an exposed stratigraphic layer of Earth's crust that is chock-full of fossils.

It is important to remember that the age of rocks exposed at the surface will not always be the same. This is because of the changing nature of Earth's crust. Parts of the continental plates have buckled, folded, sunk, and risen over millions of years. This means that different stratigraphic layers, of different ages, will be exposed in different places around the planet. Within these different layers are the fossils of organisms that lived during those times. The remains of dinosaurs are not found in the rugged terrain of northeastern Pennsylvania, for example. The rocks there date from a time other than that of the dinosaurs. But one can find there the remains of some of the first vertebrates to walk onto land many millions of years before the dinosaurs. Similarly, in the splendid fossil layers of finely grained limestone in Bavaria, one may find the fossils of the first bird, *Archaeopteryx*, but not the remains of wooly mammoths that walked through Asia and Europe a hundred million years later. Each layer of the Earth dates from a particular prehistoric time, and only certain organisms will be found in a given layer.

Where, then, is the best place to find fossils? Although fossils are sometimes discovered by accident, most are found by people who know what they are looking for. They begin by going to a place where a fossil-bearing layer of the Earth is exposed. This is quite often a dry, exposed area called a badlands. Little rain falls on badlands, and there are few trees and plants to obscure exposed layers of sedimentary rock. This makes it easier to discover fossils poking out from the rock. Major badlands of the Earth in which fossil vertebrates of all types have been found include the Great Plains and Rocky Mountain regions of the United States; Alberta, Canada; Mongolia, in Central Asia; North Africa; and the Patagonia region of South America. These are by no means the only place that fossils are found, but they have yielded tons of mammal and dinosaur bones over the years.

Relative dating is the most common technique used to determine the age of a fossil. Fossils are generally found in layers of the Earth for which the age is already known. Sometimes the layers of the Earth are difficult to identify with certainty. In such cases, a paleontologist either looks for other fossils known to have been found in a given layer before or may try a form of absolute dating if the fossil material permits.

FOSSILS AND THE VULNERABILITY OF SPECIES

Fossils reveal the many kinds of life that once existed on the planet. They also illustrate the inescapable truth that species do not last forever. Even the most successful lines of organisms one day become extinct.

The study of prehistoric life is also about the geologic and biologic events that lead to the demise of species. Some species disappear over a long period of time, while others reach their end in the flash of a cataclysmic geologic event. To learn about extinctions is to come face to face with the kinds of threats that may one day affect humans and other creatures in the world today.

SUMMARY

This chapter described the types of fossils and how they are made, explored the environmental and geologic circumstances that make fossils possible, and discussed the remarkable kinds of information that fossils reveal about past life.

1. Fossils are the paleontologist's key to understanding prehistoric life.
2. Fossils represent any physical trace of past life.
3. Only a tiny fraction of past life has been fossilized.
4. To become a fossil, an organism must die and then be buried quickly by sediment such as sand, mud, volcanic ash, or other material. The body then is covered by additional layers of sediment over time until a rock is formed, encasing the fossil.
5. Once buried, the body of an organism can remain undisturbed for long periods of time, even millions of years.
6. The process of mineralization transforms body parts—including bones, blood, tissue, and organs—from organic material to a combination of bone and stone.
7. Types of fossils include body fossils, molds and casts, carbon film impressions, mummified remains, preservation in amber, frozen carcasses, and trace fossils.
8. Fossil bones and body parts provide many clues to the anatomy of an organism.
9. Skeletal features are also a key to the physiology of an organism: the study of body functions such as eating, running, fighting, mating, foraging, and other tasks needed to survive.

10. Natural circumstances affecting the chances for fossilization include an organism's population, anatomy, size, and biology and habitat.

11. Fossils are usually found where a known fossil-bearing layer of the Earth is exposed.

4

EXTINCTION

For many species of organisms, the ability to survive and adapt to ever-changing environmental conditions ensures their longevity throughout the ages. Nature does not, however, grant the survival of a species forever. There are times when even the hardiest of species fail to survive a gradual or sudden modification to their habitat. The fossil record confirms the fact that no species lasts forever. Every species eventually becomes extinct.

The nature and causes of extinction are explored in this chapter. Extinction is a normal process affected by the biological traits of an organism as well as by external, physical conditions of the world around the organism. In the flow of life on Earth, extinction irrevocably denies the continuance of some species while creating new opportunities for those left behind.

UNDERSTANDING EXTINCTION

Fossils greatly puzzled those who first tried to explain them. Theophrastus (c. 372 B.C.–c. 287 B.C.) was a botanical student of Aristotle (384 B.C.–322 B.C.). Theophrastus thought that fossils were a kind of seed that sprouted after having been buried by sediment. Although his understanding of fossil making was later proved incorrect, Theophrastus made a significant connection by linking fossils to naturally occurring layers of Earth's crust. Little was understood about the true origin and age of fossils until the science of geology began to explain the nature of sedimentary deposits.

The biggest puzzle of all was the nature of the organisms seen in fossils. They appeared to represent the remains of long-dead organisms. Some of these organisms were familiar, such as fossil leaves and seashells. Many other fossils, however, revealed creatures that were wildly different from anything known to still be alive. Early attempts by explorers, natural scientists, and educators to explain away fossils come up laughingly short when they are compared to what is currently known. In 1663, Otto von Güricke (1602–1686), physicist and burgomaster of Magdeburg, Germany, cobbled together the remains of a prehistoric elephant and declared that they were the bones of a unicorn. One of the tusks served as the mythical creature's horn. Similar cases of mistaken identity were made throughout the eighteenth century in Europe and America, largely because of ignorance about the past, lack of knowledge about the longevity of life on Earth, and the heretical nature of the idea that some of God's organisms may have perished forever through no fault of their own.

With advances in geological thought in the early nineteenth century and the discovery of more and more fossilized organisms, scientists realized that many kinds of animals that had been alive in the past were no longer alive in the present. This led to the fantastic idea that species could become extinct.

Extinction is the irreversible elimination of an entire species of plant or animal. Extinction occurs because a species cannot adapt effectively to changes in its environment. These changes may be caused by physical changes to the Earth and climate or the rise of better adapted competition, or may have biological causes such as disease. In the modern world, one hears about endangered species such as whales, pandas, and condors. These are species that are close to becoming extinct for a variety of reasons.

The concept of a species is important to an understanding of extinction. A species is a category of organisms that is capable of interbreeding and that produces offspring that can also reproduce. Plants and animals all have species. Species is the most basic unit of classification.

Extinction relates to the disappearance of an entire species, not just individual members of a species population. For example, dogs are a species of mammal. If all dogs found in South America suddenly died of a terrible disease, the species of dog would not become extinct because it would have surviving members in other parts of the world. If all dogs in the world died due to such a disease, however, and no dogs were left to reproduce, then the species of dog would be considered extinct.

Extinction is a natural process. Under favorable conditions, species of plants and animals exist for between 1 million and 10 million years. After that, most species evolve into another species or disappear entirely, becoming extinct. With life having existed on Earth for about 3.5 billion years, it can be seen that many kinds of creatures have come and gone. Today, there are as many as 40 million different species of plants and animals. This is nothing, however, when compared to the whole history of life on Earth. During the past 3.5 billion years, between 5 billion and 50 *billion* species have existed at one time or another. With only about one-tenth of 1 percent of those species still alive today, this means that 99.9 percent of all the species of organisms that have ever lived are now extinct. If extinct species could be measured using tennis balls, it would take a sphere the size of the Moon to hold 1.5 billion of them. That is an estimate on the low side of how many species have gone extinct in Earth's history.

What if species never died out? Imagine a world in which extinction did not exist. If every species that ever evolved was still around, the planet would be overcrowded with species competing for smaller and smaller niches in the habitat. There would probably be a snag in evolution, with no room for new species. If dinosaurs had not become extinct, there is no telling how smart they would have become. If dinosaurs had continued to rule, they may have made it difficult for mammals to rise with such success. In a world so changed, humans may never have arisen. These intriguing speculations are made obsolete by extinction. When nature rolls the dice, many species can fall.

Extinctions are brought about by many factors. The fact that the dinosaurs eventually died out does not mean that they were stupid or inadequate. The fact that the wooly mammoths disappeared doesn't mean that they took a wrong turn at the North Pole. One thing is certain: Species become extinct through no fault of their own. Species can disappear for a variety of biological and physical reasons. Some extinctions take long periods of geologic time, while others happen in a flash of the fossil record.

THE HUMAN FACTOR

The influence of humans on extinctions is also worth noting before exploring the broader categories of extinctions that have existed since people walked the Earth. Thanks to their problem-solving intelligence and creation of technology, humans are the most adapt-

THINK ABOUT IT

The Longevity of Genera and Species

The first forms of life arose about 3.5 billion years ago. The history of the human species is short when compared to the longevity of many life-forms that came before humans. A favorite example for comparison is the dinosaurs, a group of related animals that dominated life on the land for 160 million years—even more if one includes their descendants, the birds, which are still alive today. Not all of the kinds of dinosaurs existed at the same time over this long period, but among the dinosaurs were families of closely related species, such as the tyrannosaurs, that lasted for 3 million to 4 million years before becoming extinct. Many other kinds of vertebrates—animals with backbones—enjoy similar success, including sharks, some lobe-finned fishes (the coelacanths), crocodiles, frogs, baleen whales, and others. All of these creatures existed, or continue to exist, in a form that dates back a million years or more. Modern humans have another 700,000 years to go before they reach the one-million-year milestone in vertebrate success. The table on page 83 shows some of the longest-standing vertebrate groups compared to humans.

able organisms ever to inhabit the Earth. They can subsist on a wide variety of foods, migrate rapidly, protect themselves from a range of climate conditions, and fabricate sophisticated tools and materials to adapt to changing physical and climatic conditions. A crocodile caught in a freakish ice storm would soon freeze to death, but a human caught in cold weather simply puts on a warm coat.

Humans affect the survival of other species directly and indirectly. As skilled predators, humans have reduced the numbers

LONGEVITY OF VERTEBRATE GENERA

Many vertebrate genera have a history lasting millions of years. Humans are not one of them. If the success of a genera can be measured by how long the genera of that species appear in the fossil record, humans have a long way to go to match the evolutionary success of these other animals.

Vertebrate Genus	First Appearance in the Fossil Record	Longevity of Genus (Millions of Years)
Trilobites	Early Cambrian Epoch	295
Coelacanths (lobe-finned fish)	Middle Devonian Epoch	390
Sharks	Late Devonian Epoch	375
Lizards	Late Permian Epoch	253
Frogs	Early Triassic Epoch	250
Turtles and tortoises	Late Triassic Epoch	203
Crocodiles	Early Jurassic Epoch	190
Newts and salamanders	Late Jurassic Epoch	150
Baleen whales	Early Oligocene Epoch	33
Bats	Early Eocene Epoch	48
Birds of prey	Middle Eocene Epoch	40
Apes	Early Miocene Epoch	20
Walruses	Late Miocene Epoch	6
Hominids (human ancestors)	Late Miocene Epoch	5.4
Modern humans	Middle Pleistocene Epoch	0.3 (300,000 years)

of many other species, sometimes through reckless overhunting. At other times, changes that human incursions have brought to a given environment have led to species extinctions. In recorded history, the extinction of the dodo was clearly caused by humans. The last of the dodoes—giant, flightless birds once found on the island of Mauritius, in the Indian Ocean—perished sometime in the late seventeenth century. Some dodoes were hunted for their meat, but many more seem to have died because their forest habitat and food supply were destroyed by human activities, and because animals such as cats, rats, and pigs that came to the island with humans preyed on the eggs in the dodoes' ground-level nests. In recent times, overhunting continues to threaten the existence of mammals such as gorillas and elephants.

Overhunting by humans is not restricted to periods of recorded history. Mammoths, mastodons, and their many elephant cousins once roamed the five major continents of the Earth. By 10,000 years ago, however, all but a few species were driven into extinction everywhere but in sub-Saharan Africa and South Asia. While these extinctions were due in part to dramatic climate changes, a recent study published by the National Academy of Sciences showed a strong correlation between the spread of early humans and the disappearance of mammoths and their kin. The verdict was clear to anthropologist Todd Surovell of the University of Wyoming, who led the study. After examining evidence from 41 fossil sites in Africa, Asia, Europe, and the Americas, he and his colleagues could see that when early humans spread from Africa to the other continents, they left telltale signs of elephant hunting along the way. Elephants were especially susceptible to overhunting because of their large size and small number of offspring. That only three, possibly 4, species of elephants still exist can also be explained by their degree of interaction with humans. "The elephant populations that have managed to survive," explained Surovell, "live in areas where humans have never settled in large numbers."

Through sheer aggression, humans may have also been responsible for killing off another species of humans, *Homo neanderthalensis*, better known simply as the Neandertals. These relatives of ancient humans last walked the Earth with *Homo sapiens* about

30,000 years ago. Whether *Homo sapiens* actually killed off Neandertals is not known. What *is* known is that *Homo sapiens* moved into Europe, where the Neandertals lived, and displaced them until the Neandertal population dwindled to extinction.

The remarkable ability of humans to adapt the environment for their own needs—to build shelters, cities, factories, and highways and make other significant changes to the habitat—sometimes detrimentally affects other species indirectly. As may have been the case with the ill-fated dodo, this can result in the extinction of plants and animals. The United States government enacted the Endangered Species Act in 1973 to protect species of plants and animals whose numbers had been reduced nearly to the point of extinction. Many of these organisms have been adversely affected by habitat changes brought about by human endeavors. In recognizing the fragility of species, the Endangered Species Act also acknowledges the responsibility of people to look after and protect other species of life that are unable to protect themselves from extinction.

BACKGROUND EXTINCTIONS

A **background extinction** is the kind of quiet extinction that happens all the time. It is a kind of extinction that affects only one species at a time. There are no headlines about background extinctions. No blockbuster movies. No big names. But most of the extinctions that have ever taken place could be called background extinctions. Background extinctions may occur suddenly or slowly over a long period. The causes and extent of background extinctions are governed by the relationship between a species and the environment in which it thrives.

Organisms are adapted to live fruitfully in a given habitat. The fate of an organism lies in its ability to survive and reproduce under given conditions in its environment. Sometimes a species becomes extinct because it gradually changes into a newer, fitter species over time. The history of the horse in North America offers many good examples of earlier species being replaced by fitter new species. The earliest members of the North American horse species date back more than 34 million years. *Hyracotherium*, the first horse species, was only about two feet (60 cm) long. This early horse had a mouthful of teeth that were only suited for eating the soft leaves found in low-growing tropical plants. Its feet had four toes on the **forelimbs** and three on the **hind limbs**. *Hyracotherium* probably browsed under the cover of low-growing trees and bushes. Over many millions of years, horses with traits that allowed them to run faster, grow bigger, and eat a wider variety of plants, such as grasses, gradually changed into newer, bigger, faster species that were at home on the wide-open plain. As a result, modern horses run on one broadened toe, or hoof, on each foot and have broader and harder teeth than earlier horses. The smaller *Hyracotherium* horse species became extinct.

Background extinction can also occur suddenly. A species can become extinct when its biology cannot adapt quickly enough to rapid changes in its habitat. Consider Australia's koala. Its digestive system, unique among mammals, has adapted so that it can survive mostly by eating the leaves of eucalyptus trees. While this restricts the koala's geographic range to eucalyptus forests, its special adaptation means that it has little competition for food. The koala's reliance on eucalyptus also puts the animal's future in a precarious situation. If a blight or sudden change in climate wiped out Australia's eucalyptus forests, the koala could disappear, too, because its biology is not readily adaptable to the digestion of other kinds of plants.

In the annals of prehistory, gradual background extinctions were often triggered by geologic changes in the restless Earth. Volcanic action was widespread during many past geologic eras. So, too, were dramatic changes in Earth's crust. Continents were joined and then separated again. Oceans formed and then closed again. The amount of land or sea available to support life sometimes changed dramatically over millions of years. These changes had deadly effects on some forms of life whose habitat was gradually wiped out. Many past species were unable to adapt to their slowly changing world.

Background extinctions triggered by gradual changes in the environment may require millions of years to unfold. These changes are so slow that they are sometimes barely perceptible in the fossil record. On average, a species evolves and dies off about every four million years. Background extinctions result in about 10 to 25 percent of all species dying off every million years. At the opposite end of the extinction scale is the sudden or catastrophic extinction. This is a natural event so terrible and devastating that it takes place in a geological split second lasting anywhere from several years to a million years.

MASS EXTINCTIONS

Sometimes the cause of an extinction is so vast and so sudden that hundreds, maybe thousands, of species are affected. A rapid change of this nature that wipes out significant numbers of species is called a **mass extinction.** Compared to background extinctions, which may take several million years to occur for a given species, a mass extinction will kill off more than 25 percent of all species in a million years or less.

Mass extinctions are the kind of extinctions that change the direction of nearly all life on the planet. The end of the age of dinosaurs was one such extinction because it killed off not only dinosaurs, but also a large percentage of other land and sea organisms at the same time. Mass extinctions are devastating to life and are marked by a point in the geological record when previously dominant life-forms entirely disappear. The divisions between eras in the geological record are often divided by mass extinctions. This is one way to acknowledge the significant difference between fossils found before and after the period of extinction. Mass extinctions are named after the geologic time span affected by them. This is often the borderline between two periods. For example, the name Cretaceous-Tertiary extinction denotes that the extinction occurred at the end of the Cretaceous Period and marked the beginning of the Tertiary Period that followed.

Mass extinctions have many causes and are often the result of multiple, accumulating natural disasters. Even mass extinctions take a long time to unravel Earth's ecosystem—perhaps as long as a million years in some cases. The causes are not always as sudden as one might first think, but they generally involved a widespread change to the environment and stability of Earth's crust.

The worst mass extinction of all time climaxed 251 million years ago at the end of the Permian Period. The extinction was triggered by a prolonged period of massive volcanic eruptions lasting several hundred thousand years. Massive flows of lava, centered in what is today Siberia, probably caused global warming and a runaway greenhouse effect that lasted thousands of years. This caused climate changes that affected plant and animal life on land and in the sea. There were also dramatic shifts in Earth's crust during this period that affected ocean levels and the habitats of all organisms. The final blows came when the Earth was struck by at least two asteroids. The heat, debris, and deadly chemicals thrown into the atmosphere from the volcanoes polluted the air and oceans, causing widespread unbalance in the land and sea ecosystems. The oceans sank to their lowest levels in the last 545 million years. These factors combined to create a worldwide environmental crisis for most life-forms. The Permian-Triassic extinction killed 68 percent of species of life on the planet. The seas were especially hard hit. One reason was that many of the habitats occupied by bottom-living, shallow-dwelling creatures disappeared. Many species of small-fish eaters, corals, and all trilobites disappeared at that time. On land, the victims included small insect-eaters, large plant-eaters, and the top carnivores. By comparison, the Cretaceous-Tertiary extinction, whose victims included the dinosaurs, killed about 42 percent of the world's species of plants and animals.

The most likely villains behind mass extinctions include the following:

- Shifts in Earth's crust. Movement of tectonic plates can greatly affect the habitat of species. For example, expanses of water prevent species from traveling between their disconnected landmasses. When nature builds bridges between landmasses, the inhabitants can suddenly intermingle. This always results in the loss of species due to competition for the same ecological niches.

- Climate changes (hot and cold). If the average temperature of a habitat drops, even by only a few degrees, and this change is sustained for months or years, it can severely affect the plants and animals that live there.
- Massive and continuous volcanic eruptions. Volcanic action during prehistoric times was sometimes more violent and sustained than anything experienced today. Long periods of volcanic eruption not only affected organisms living near the eruptions, but also could poison the atmosphere, produce smoke that could block sunlight, and change climates all over the Earth. The volcanic activity that occurred in what is now Siberia at the end of Permian Period lasted from between 500,000 and 800,000 years.
- Changes in the chemistry of air and water. Volcanic eruptions and asteroid strikes spewed forth pulverized minerals whose chemical composition became part of the air breathed by organisms.
- Asteroid or comet strikes. The aftereffects of a collision with a large body from space might have been long-lasting. Among the problems that scientists believe could have been caused by such collisions are widespread fires, tsunamis (if the strike occurred in the ocean), air pollution, blockage of the Sun by soot and smoke, and dramatic changes in temperature.

Asteroids as a Culprit

There is growing evidence that many mass extinctions were triggered by collisions of asteroids and comets with Earth. This idea was first suggested in 1980 by a research team led by Nobel Prize–winning physicist Luis Alvarez (1911–1988) and his geologist son Walter Alvarez (b. 1940) at the University of California, Berkeley. While studying stratigraphic layers in Italy, the Alvarez team noticed a thin, barely noticeable layer of clay deposited about 65 million years ago at the end of the Cretaceous Period. Analysis of the clay revealed that it contained 30 times the concentration of the mineral iridium than is normally found in layers of the Earth.

Knowing that such high levels of iridium have also been found in asteroids, the Alvarez team theorized that the deposit was the result of a severe collision of an asteroid with Earth. The Alvarez finding has since been corroborated by the discovery of many other locations around the Earth that feature high concentrations of iridium dating from the end of the Cretaceous Period. The fact that this proposed asteroid hit coincided with the mass extinction of the dinosaurs made the theory that much more intriguing. Not only had the Alvarez team identified a major culprit in the demise of the most popular of all prehistoric creatures, they had introduced a possible new mechanism behind mass-extinction events.

Just how an asteroid strike might trigger a mass extinction is a lesson in the global effects of natural disasters. In 1983, Luis Alvarez explained it this way: "When the asteroid hit, it threw up a great cloud of dust that quickly circled the globe. It is now seen worldwide, typically as a clay layer a few centimeters thick in which we see a relatively high concentration of the element iridium." This cloud of smoke was hot and probably full of burning ash at first, setting fires worldwide and blocking sunlight for weeks or months. The result was a gradual diminishment of plant life and the gradual death of organisms that fed on plants and predators that fed on the plant eaters.

As attractive as it was, the Alvarez theory alone did not prove definitively that asteroids had killed off the last of the dinosaurs. The Alvarez team had identified the "smoke," behind the asteroid collision, but not the "gun." The remnants of iridium left in the Italian clay was not found at the site of the asteroid hit. Instead, this layer of iridium-rich clay was the residue of a distant explosion that filled Earth's atmosphere with smoke and ash for months—but because iridium can also be produced from within the Earth and released through violent volcanic eruptions, the jury was still out on the asteroid theory until further evidence was found. What geologists needed to find to support the theory was the location of a corresponding asteroid strike, known as an **impact crater**.

The collision of an asteroid with Earth big enough to cause a mass extinction would have left behind a sizable impact crater

in the crust of the planet—a crater that probably measured 50 or
more miles (31 km) in diameter. There are many curious, crater-
like geologic features on Earth, but not all of them are the result
of a collision with an extraterrestrial object. Some are natural land
formations or were caused by prolonged volcanic activity in the
deep past. Other physical clues are needed to determine whether a
crater was made by a large impact. Those clues come in the form
of shocked quartz and tektites found in a crater. Shocked quartz
is an unusual form of quartz that has been structurally altered by
extreme pressure, such as that made by the impact of a meteorite
with sand in Earth's crust. Tektites are a form of roughly hewn
beads of natural glass also created under great pressure possibly
when an asteroid strikes Earth. The combination of high levels of
iridium, shocked quartz, and tektites produces the "smoking gun"
that geologists look for in identifying an impact crater. If the age of
an impact crater is close to that of a major depletion of species in
the fossil record, then an asteroid hit becomes a likely contributor
to a mass-extinction event.

Geologists have been combing the surface of Earth for craters
that serve as the telltale signs of asteroid strikes, but the smoking
gun is not always easy to find. Some of these craters are hidden
under the oceans or obscured by vegetation, making them difficult
to spot even with help from satellite imagery. Some craters from
long ago may have also been broken up by later shifting of the crust,
thus making the task of recognizing them even more difficult.

The breakthrough for the Alvarez theory came in 1990. Gradu-
ate geology student Alan R. Hildebrand (b. 1955) was exploring rock
layers in Haiti and the Yucatan Peninsula of Mexico for evidence
of ancient tsunamis. After he found quantities of iridium, shocked
quartz, and tektites at various locations in the area, he turned his
attention to the idea that an impact crater was located in the region.
A petroleum engineer named Glen T. Penfield had come to a similar
conclusion some 10 years earlier while investigating the makeup of
oil drill cores from the Yucatan. Backed by Penfield's earlier findings, a group of scientists led by Hildebrand and Penfield announced

in 1991 that they had identified the most likely candidate for the "crater of doom" that led to the demise of the dinosaurs. Now called the Chicxulub crater for a nearby town, the remains of the crater are found along the northern coast of the Yucatan Peninsula, straddling the land and sea. Chicxulub is a large geologic feature measuring 283 miles (170 km) in diameter. The asteroid that caused this crater was about six miles (10 km) across. Another asteroid or comet may have struck the Earth at about the same time, but the location of that body's crater is still in dispute.

Asteroids now have been implicated in three of the top five mass-extinction events recorded in the fossil record. In some cases, an asteroid strike alone may not have been the cause of a mass extinction. These massive killings were made worse by a combination of natural catastrophes. The Cretaceous-Tertiary extinction of the last dinosaurs was caused in part by Earth's being struck by an unusually large asteroid or comet. The impact of this strike was a shock to the planet but may also have triggered enormous volcanic eruptions in what is today India. The combination of asteroid hits and volcanic action led to blazing forest fires, sending dense smoke into the atmosphere for months, even years. The effect on Earth's habitats was monumental. The chemistry of both air and water was probably changed for a long period of time, perhaps proving as lethal to the planet's inhabitants as the loss of sunlight and change in climate.

Some scientists looking at the evidence for mass extinctions in Earth's geologic record have noted that there appears to be a repeating pattern of mass demise. According to these scientists, there is a cycle of mass extinctions in which such an extinction occurs every 26 million years. This cycle can be sketched out in the geologic record, but the evidence is not complete. While the cause for such a repeating pattern cannot be proved with certainty, some scientists have proposed that Earth is bombarded every 26 million years by a "cloud" of comets that orbits some unknown celestial body—a distant planet too dim to see or a companion star to our Sun. This theory lends even more credence to the possibility that Earth's ecosystem is occasionally devastated by crashing comets and asteroids.

Major Mass Extinctions

The history of mass extinctions is punctuated by five especially large disasters for life on the planet. The evidence for these extinctions comes from noticeable drops in the numbers of species found in the fossil record and from geologic evidence for life-altering natural disasters. These extinctions were so devastating to life on Earth that their locations in the planet's sedimentary layers have been used to mark the starting and ending points of several major spans of the geologic timescale.

Cambrian-Ordovician Extinction (485 million years ago). About 42 percent of all known species perished. This killing primarily affected ocean life and may have been caused by tectonic plate shifts and volcanic eruptions that caused a drop in sea level. Brachiopods, conodonts (eel-like marine invertebrates), and trilobites suffered heavy species loss.

Ordovician-Silurian Extinction (440 million years ago). About 85 percent of all known marine species perished. This extinction primarily affected ocean life. It may have been due in part to glaciation, an ice age in which huge ice sheets took up water from the oceans and lowered sea levels. Trilobites, echinoderms, and nautiloids suffered great species losses.

Permian-Triassic Extinction (248 millions years ago). About 95 percent of all known ocean species and 75 percent of terrestrial species perished. Land vertebrates also suffered hard, losing about three quarters of their species. This extinction was caused by a combination of asteroid hits and tremendous volcanic action, resulting in greatly lowered sea levels and changes to worldwide habitats.

Triassic-Jurassic Extinction (208 million years ago). About 45 percent of all known marine and terrestrial species perished. In what was possibly an accumulation of closely spaced smaller extinction events, species of both land and sea suffered considerably. Sponges and brachiopods were hard hit, and all species of conodonts disappeared. On land, insects, early amphibians, and other early vertebrates died out, making way for the dinosaurs that followed. Increased rainfall, volcanic eruptions, and possible aster-oid collisions are the leading culprits for this extinction.

Cretaceous-Tertiary Extinction (65 million years ago). About 43 percent of all known marine and terrestrial species perished. This most famous of all extinctions did not earn its reputation by being the most devastating—the Permian-Triassic extinction has that distinc-tion—but it is famous because it wiped out the dinosaurs. Not only dinosaurs were lost, however. Most marine reptiles, flying reptiles, many plants, and the long-enduring ammonites were lost. This extinc-tion was more sudden than most though. It appears to be the result of a combination of massive asteroid collisions and subsequent volcanic activity that vastly altered the climate of Earth for many years.

THE GOOD NEWS ABOUT EXTINCTIONS

Life on Earth has been doing battle with extinction since the exis-tence of the first species. The survival of a species is governed by two great natural forces. The ability to adapt gradually through bio-logical variation to a changing habitat allows some species to persist longer than others. This ability to adapt also has a downside: Some organisms become overly specialized for a particular life and habitat and so become doomed to replacement by more adaptable species. The result is the background extinction of a species.

The other great force—the flip side of background extinction—is the mass extinction, the sudden and catastrophic wiping out of many species at the same time. Even the most successful lines of organisms can perish suddenly when an enormous environmental catastrophe makes it impossible for them to recover through the natural course of adaptation. Through the mechanisms of background extinctions and mass extinctions, the natural world maintains a balance of liv-ing species kept in check by environmental conditions.

Extinction happens to all species sooner or later. What is bad news for one species, however, is good news for others. Mass extinc-tions open up niches in the ecosystem for other organisms to fill. When the Triassic-Jurassic extinction wiped out the largest preda-tory creatures of the time, the first dinosaurs were waiting in the wings. They quickly spread across the world, leading a robust pro-

MAJOR MASS EXTINCTIONS

Extinction Event	Millions of Years Ago (MYA)	Extent	Cause	Most Dramatic Casualties
Cambrian-Ordovician Extinction	485	About 42 percent of marine animal species perished.	Tectonic plate shifts, volcanic eruptions, drop in sea level.	Brachiopods, conodonts, and trilobites
Ordovician-Silurian Extinction	440	About 85 percent of marine animal species perished.	Glaciation and lower sea levels	Trilobites, echinoderms, and nautiloids
Permian-Triassic Extinction	248	About 95 percent of marine animal species and 75 percent of terrestrial animal species perished.	Asteroid hits, volcanic action, and lower sea levels	96 percent of all ocean species; 75 percent of land vertebrates
Triassic-Jurassic Extinction	208	About 45 percent of all known species perished.	Increased rainfall, volcanic eruptions, and possible asteroid hits	In the ocean, sponges and brachiopods suffered heavily and all species of conodonts disappeared. On land, insects, early amphibians, and other early vertebrates died out.
Cretaceous-Tertiary Extinction	65	About 43 percent of all known species perished.	Massive asteroid hits and subsequent volcanic activity	All dinosaurs (except birds), marine reptiles, and flying reptiles and ammonites perished; many plants were lost.

cession of vertebrates and becoming the dominant vertebrates on the planet for more than 160 million years. They were the most successful large-bodied creatures ever to walk the Earth. When the end came for the dinosaurs about 65 million years ago, however, small but adaptable mammals were waiting for their turn in the spotlight. Mammals soon grew large and diverse and filled the plant-eating and meat-eating niches once occupied by the dinosaurs. Humans eventually stepped into the star's spot as the most intelligent and perhaps most adaptable of all creatures. Despite its current longevity, however, the time at the top for humans is a mere moment in the history of Earth. Humans and their closest ancestors have at least 155 million years to go to achieve the success of the dinosaurs.

Changes to the environment do not always result in the extinction of a species. The persistence of animals such as sharks, birds, turtles, and crocodiles for many millions of years is a testament to their hardy biological traits. How species adapt to changing conditions in their world can ensure their resistance to extinction and is governed by evolution.

SUMMARY

This chapter explored the nature and causes of extinction.

1. Extinction is the irreversible elimination of an entire species of plant or animal.
2. A species is a category of organisms that is capable of interbreeding and that produces offspring that can also reproduce. Species is the most basic unit in the scientific classification of life.
3. Extinction is a normal and natural process, but it may be accelerated by humans' encroachment on the habitat of other organisms.
4. A species can become extinct when its biology cannot adapt quickly enough to rapid changes in its habitat.
5. A background extinction is a kind of quiet extinction that is happening all of the time. A background extinction generally happens slowly over a long period of time and affects only one species at a time.
6. A mass extinction is a rapid extinction caused by far-reaching changes to a wide environment. A mass extinction will kill off more than 25 percent of all species in a million years or less.
7. Mass extinctions may be caused by shifts in Earth's crust, climate changes, massive and continuous volcanic eruptions, changes in the chemistry of air and water, asteroid and comet strikes, or a combination of such events.
8. There have been five big extinction events in Earth's history.
9. There is considerable evidence that an asteroid strike was at least partly responsible for the extinction of the last of the dinosaurs at the boundary of the Cretaceous and Tertiary Periods.
10. Extinction leads to opportunities for other organisms to thrive.

SECTION THREE:
How Life Develops and Its Classification

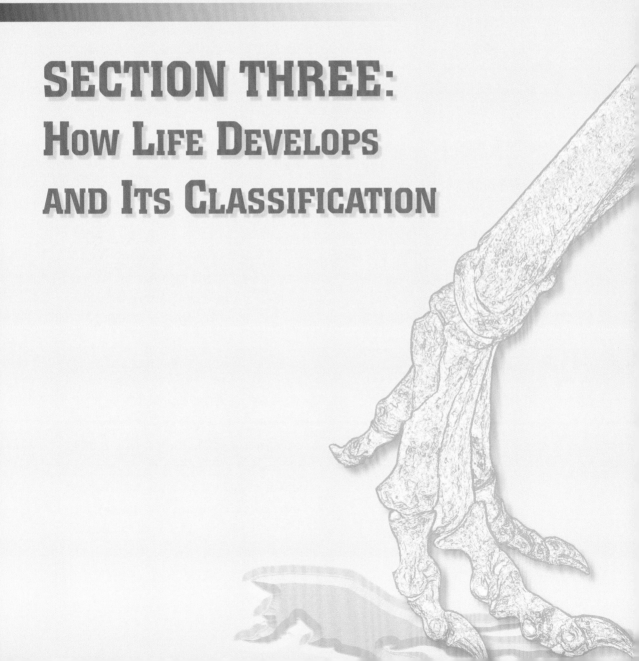

5

LIFE AND EVOLUTION

At one time, there was no life on Earth. The incredible number and variety of plants, animals, and other organisms known today and seen in the fossil record evolved gradually beginning about 3.5 billion years ago. The earliest life-forms were single-celled organisms. Those organisms led to the development of more complex, multicellular plants and animals. The natural process behind the development of new species is called evolution.

This chapter explores the basic characteristics of life and the process of evolution that continues to help life adapt to ever-changing conditions in the world. The historically important concepts of **natural selection** and **adaptation**, introduced in 1859 by Charles Darwin, are the underlying forces of evolution. These phenomena are explained in this chapter along with current scientific evidence for evolution from the study of **molecular** biology and **genetics**, two fields of study that were unknown in Darwin's time.

WHAT IS LIFE?

We instinctively know when something is alive. One rarely confuses an inorganic object with a living thing. Anyone can tell that a cat running down the street is alive and a motorcycle is not. But what are the reasons behind this deduction? One cannot reason that "the cat is alive because it moves," because a motorcycle can also move. One cannot conclude that "the cat is alive because it eats," because a motorcycle, too, can consume fuel. Yet a motorcycle is clearly not alive because it fails to share a set of five basic attributes exhibited by all organisms. These characteristics are:

1. Organisms are composed of one or more cells. Cells are the basic building blocks of living things. Every cell is contained by an outer membrane that separates the cell from its surrounding environment. There are many kinds of cells, and within each are complex molecules that carry out the fundamental functions of living.

2. Life can store and expend energy. Being alive means that an organism can get energy and nutrients from the outside, convert outside energy and nutrients into its own energy, release waste, and grow. The combination of these functions is called **metabolism.** Breathing, eating, and going to the bathroom are all metabolic functions.

3. Life responds to stimuli. Changes in the environment cause an organism to react in behavioral, metabolic, and physiological ways. Behavior might change, as when an animal seeks shelter from the cold. An organism's metabolism might change, as when a bear's bodily functions slow down during hibernation. In addition, an organism's physiology might change, as when a dog sheds hair during the summer to remain cooler or a plant leans toward the Sun to catch more light.

4. Organisms can reproduce. Creating other organisms of the same kind is a unique trait of living things. To reproduce is to create a kind of copy of oneself. Without the ability to reproduce, a species would disappear. Reproduction passes along hereditary molecules to the offspring, ensuring the continuance of the species.

5. Living things maintain a condition of biological stability. A dog is always a dog, a leaf is always a leaf. Living things follow the rules set forth in their DNA to become and maintain whatever they are. This maintenance of biological stability goes on regardless of what happens to the environment around a living thing. The metabolism and structures of living things are self-regulated to maintain a state of **homeostasis,** the biological stability of living things.

The Five Traits of All Organisms

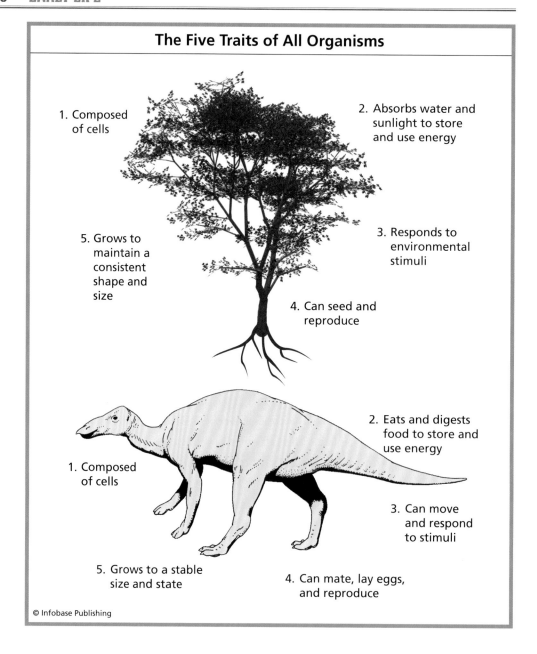

1. Composed of cells

2. Absorbs water and sunlight to store and use energy

5. Grows to maintain a consistent shape and size

3. Responds to environmental stimuli

4. Can seed and reproduce

2. Eats and digests food to store and use energy

1. Composed of cells

3. Can move and respond to stimuli

5. Grows to a stable size and state

4. Can mate, lay eggs, and reproduce

All organisms, no matter how widely diverse—from a single-celled bacterium to a blue whale, or from a human to a strand of seaweed—share all five of those essential traits.

Fossils are clues to the nature of extinct life. Although what is known about past life begins with merely an impression in the rock

THINK ABOUT IT

Is It Alive?

Using the five traits of living things as your test, explain why each of the following things is either alive or not alive. Check your ideas against the explanations included below.

    a. *A mule.* A mule is sterile and cannot reproduce. Is it alive? Why or why not?

    b. *Fire.* Fire "eats" and "breathes." It consumes fuel and converts it to heat. Fire consumes oxygen, as do living and breathing organisms. Fire responds to stimuli such as wind and water. It can grow. Fire can maintain a state of stability if given certain conditions, such as a fireplace full of burning logs. Fire can die out. It can reproduce itself by throwing sparks that can start other fires. Why, despite all these attributes, is fire not alive?

    c. *A virus.* A virus has genetic material—nucleic acids—so that it can reproduce itself. A virus has an outer shell made up of proteins. A virus must be inside a cell to reproduce. In this way, a virus is a kind of parasite. A virus is inert when it is outside a host cell. Is a virus alive? Why or why not?

Explanations

    a. Sometimes the rules do not apply. Mules are born as the offspring of a donkey and a horse. A mule is a **hybrid,** an offspring of two animals of different varieties, breeds, or species. A mule is certainly alive in all other respects, so a mule is considered an exception to the rules that define life. On a related note, mules are not a species because they usually cannot reproduce. The only way to get a mule is to cross a horse and a donkey.

    b. The primary traits that separate fire from living things are a lack of cell structure and a lack of living metabolism. Fire does not have a way to store and maintain proteins, carbohydrates, and nucleic

(continues)

(continued)

acids within its own physical structure, although it can certainly consume them most readily!

c. A virus is not an independent living thing. A virus can become part of a living thing if it invades a cell. A virus itself does not have cells and is much smaller than a living cell. A virus's DNA, and its ability to make copies of itself, is activated only by the chemistry of the cell the virus invades. Because a virus cannot grow and cannot reproduce unless it is inside a living cell, a virus is not considered to be a living thing. Viruses can certainly make living things feel sick, however.

or some mineralized remains, it appears that past life possessed all of the five traits found in organisms today.

DOMAINS AND KINGDOMS OF LIFE

Even though all organisms share the five essential traits just explained, organisms can still be extraordinarily different from one another. One might say as different as a lily and an elephant, but even this simple contrast leads to more questions. To better understand the characteristics that distinguish one organism from another, scientists begin by grouping them into **kingdoms** representing different forms of life.

The Greek philosopher Aristotle was perhaps the first scientific thinker to make an attempt at classifying life. He divided organisms into the two kingdoms of plants and animals. Aristotle's two kingdoms stood the test of time for several centuries. Even when, in 1758, the great Swedish botanist Carolus Linnaeus (1707–1778) introduced an intricate new methodology for grouping and naming organisms, he retained the two kingdoms of plants and animals.

Linnaeus laid the groundwork for classifying all life. The Linnaean method of dividing living things into two kingdoms was based on what could be seen with the naked eye. By the late nineteenth century, biologists using light microscopes were aware that organisms were composed of cells, but the microscopes of the day could not magnify a cell greatly enough to reveal its internal structure. Most biologists, unable to see the tiny components found within a cell, assumed that each cell was a kind of grab bag of molecules. All of this changed in 1945 when Albert Claude (1899–1983) and his colleagues at the Rockefeller Institute published the first electron micrograph of an intact cell. Magnified 1,600 times, the image revealed that cells contained many small functional structures. With the door now open to the world of the cell, many biologists turned their attention to deciphering these minute structures and studying the similarities between cells found in different kinds of organisms. As a result, some startling changes took place in the definitions of life-forms.

The first great departure from the Linnaean two-kingdom system came in 1959 with the work of ecologist Robert H. Whittaker (1920–1980). Drawing on microbiology, Whittaker refined the definition of plant and animal kingdoms by considering their cellular structure. Comparing the nature of cells in different kinds of organisms, Whittaker took into account the internal components of cells and the way that cells took in nutrition. His system recognized two basic kinds of cells: those with nuclei, the **eukaryotes**, and those without nuclei, the **prokaryotes**. Whittaker then established five kingdoms of life based on the structure and function of cells. The Monera included prokaryotes, represented only by bacteria. All other organisms, the eukaryotes, were divided into four additional kingdoms based on their method of processing nutrition: Plants (using **photosynthesis**), Animals (using ingestion), and Fungi and Protists (using absorption).

Following Whittaker's innovative work, the science of microbiology continued to make significant advances, particularly in genetics. The ability to use genetic molecules, including DNA, to understand the ancestral relationships of living organisms and fossil organisms provided yet another tool for defining the kingdoms of life. DNA contains the best clues yet for accurately categorizing organisms within proper groups because it uses inherited traits to link diverse organisms with common ancestors.

Another significant discovery, in 1977, led to yet another revision of the kingdoms of life. Like Whittaker's thoughtful work, this discovery also took place in the sanctuary of a scientific laboratory. Molecular biologists Carl Woese (b. 1928) and George Fox (b. 1945) of the University of Illinois were studying the gene sequences of bacteria. While pondering samples of "bacteria" provided by a colleague, Woese and Fox discovered a form that differed substantially from other bacteria. It was an anaerobic organism, meaning that it did not require oxygen to live. Instead, it created energy by converting carbon dioxide and hydrogen to methane. This microbe was so unlike any form of life previously known that Woese and Fox considered it to be a form of life yet to be defined. The two men classified the microorganism within a new group that they called **Archaebacteria** ("ancient bacteria") to refer to its apparent ancient lineage. At the same time, Woese and Fox argued for a change in the five kingdom system of classification. Instead of five kingdoms, they proposed three **domains**—the Archaea, Bacteria, and Eukarya—to occupy a level of classification higher than the kingdom. The domain Archaea includes the archaebacteria, the domain Bacteria includes organisms having prokaryote cells other than Archaea, and the domain Eukarya includes all life with eukaryote cells. Within these three domains, Woese and Fox placed six kingdoms including Archaebacteria, their newly defined form of life within Archaea; bacteria, the only member of the domain Bacteria; and the protista, fungi, plantae, and animalia, all within the domain Eukarya. In one fell swoop, using better knowledge of the molecular structure of cells than was available to Whittaker, Woese and Fox replaced the five kingdoms of life with three domains containing six kingdoms.

Acceptance of the three-domain system was long in coming. Woese was the standard-bearer for creating three domains for the classification of life, but it was not until the 1990s that his proposed system was widely accepted. The most definitive evidence came in 1996 when the full genetic DNA sequences of Archaebacteria and Bacteria could be compared to show how different they truly were. As a result, there are now three domains, or evolutionary lineages, of life widely recognized. Even though it might technically be true that all life shares a common ancestor, none of the organisms in these three domains is considered the ancestor of an organism in another domain.

The three-domain, six kingdom system is not without its critics. Biologist Lynn Margulis (b. 1938) has written extensively in support of a modified version of Whittaker's five kingdoms. Margulis argues that the Woese system, based primarily on the molecular structure of organisms, fails to consider the whole of an organism, which in her view should include information about the molecular, **morphological** (body form and structure), and **developmental** (reproduction and growth) attributes of an organism. Despite this opposition, however, the three-domain system is widely accepted, largely because it begins with clearly definable evidence found at the base level of all organisms: the chemistry of their cells. The three domain, six-kingdom system will be the basis for any discussions of the kingdoms of life used in this book.

The three domains of life are as follows:

Bacteria. The earliest known fossils of life-forms are those of blue-green algae, bacteria dating from about 3.5 billion years ago. The **Bacteria** domain includes 6 **phyla,** or smaller divisions, of bacteria. Bacteria are single-celled organisms whose cell structure is less complex than those found in plants and animal. A bacterial cell does not have a nucleus. Instead, the cell's DNA floats freely in the cell's cytoplasm—the gelatinous fluid that fills most cells—as a tangled strand called a *nucleoid.* Even though bacteria consist only of a single cell, they are far from being simple organisms. They are one of the heartiest and most adaptable life-forms on the planet. Some bacteria can live in freezing temperatures. Others can live in liquid that is hotter than the boiling point of water. Bacteria consume a wide variety of substances for food, from mere sunlight

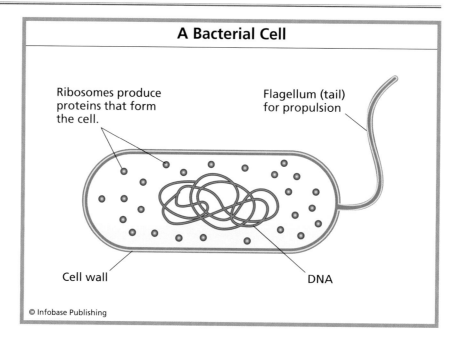

A Bacterial Cell

Ribosomes produce proteins that form the cell.

Flagellum (tail) for propulsion

Cell wall

DNA

© Infobase Publishing

to sugar, starch, and even sulfur or iron. One species of bacteria can withstand a blast of atomic radiation 1,000 times greater than would be needed to kill a human. Bacteria usually get a bad reputation because some forms can cause disease in animals and plants. Bacteria, however, are all around and serve many useful functions. Blue-green algae aid in the production of nitrogen, an element in the air that is essential for plant and animal growth. Bacteria live in the gut of living animals, helping to digest food and keeping the animals healthy. Bacteria break down decaying leaves and other organic matter, thereby returning nutrients to the soil. They also add a little tart taste to yogurt and sourdough bread.

Archaea. This group of unusual organisms probably includes the first kinds of organisms that inhabited Earth. The Archaea domain includes 4 phyla of archaebacteria. Archaebacteria live in environments that would be the harshest imaginable for other kinds of life. These prokaryotic microbes are composed of single cells and resemble bacteria, but archaebacteria are significantly different from bacteria metabolically. The ability of archaebacteria to survive without oxygen makes them unique among organisms. Their tolerance for extreme temperatures is also unusual, with some being able to live near deep ocean volcanic vents where temperatures reach 250°F (121°C). The cell structure of archaebacteria is made up of chemical building blocks different from those that make up the cell structures of bacteria and eukaryotes, and the genetic code of archaebacteria is distinct. As mentioned, archaebacteria thrive in some of the planet's more inhospitable places: hydrothermal volcanic sea vents (where superheated water squirts out through cracks in the ocean floor), salt pools, and even hot springs (where no other life-form can survive). Archaebacteria form symbiotic relationships with host organisms. Around hydrothermal sea vents, highly specialized animals including tube worms, clams, and mussels depend on archaebacteria for the absorption of nutrients from the chemically harsh seawater in which they live. These archaebacteria convert inorganic matter from vent water into food for their animal hosts. In the absence of sunlight, archaebacteria use a process called *chemosynthesis* to convert inorganic compounds such as hydrogen sulfide and carbon dioxide into energy.

Adult tubeworms living in deep-sea hydrothermal vents, where sunlight never penetrates, rely on archaebacteria to convert harsh chemicals into nutrition for them.

A Eukaryote Cell

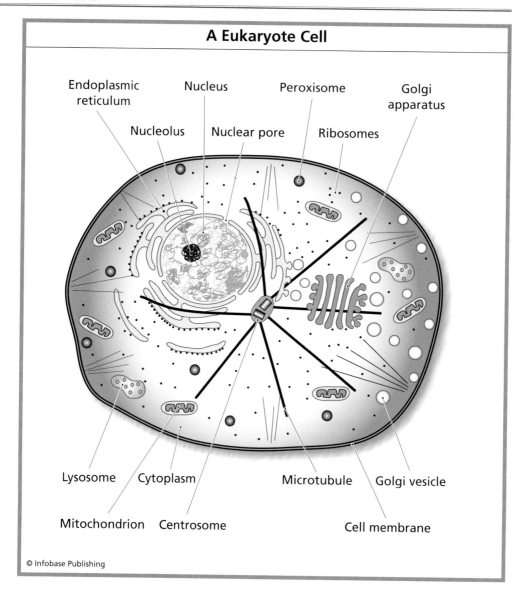

Endoplasmic reticulum · Nucleus · Peroxisome · Golgi apparatus · Nucleolus · Nuclear pore · Ribosomes · Lysosome · Cytoplasm · Microtubule · Golgi vesicle · Mitochondrion · Centrosome · Cell membrane

Eukarya. This group includes plants, animals, fungi, and protists, all with a eukaryote cell type. There are 15 phyla within the **Eukarya** domain. Considered to be more complex than single-celled Bacteria and Archaea, the multicellular Eukarya possess cells that can communicate chemically and work together, leading to the development of specialized cells within the same organism. This innovation in cell design allows multicellular organisms to build larger, more complicated bodies. It is the reason why this form of life was able to rise above its microscopic origins and build diverse organisms that are as different as ants, azaleas, anteaters, and *Apatosaurus*. This distinctive cell structure has a nucleus containing strands of DNA. The kinds of fossil organisms discussed in this book are primarily eukaryotes.

A fourth group is worth mentioning here: the **viruses.** Although one can debate whether or not viruses are actually alive—remember that they cannot reproduce by themselves, and so, fail one of the five traits associated with life—they are nonetheless important biological organisms. Viruses do not have cells. Viruses are fragments of genetic material that become activated and reproduce when

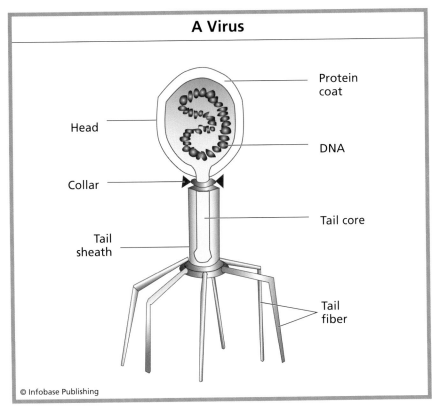

Viruses do not have cells. They are fragments of genetic material that become activated and reproduce when they come in contact with the cell of a living organism.

they come in contact with the cell of another organism. Viruses are responsible for many familiar diseases, including chicken pox, influenza, smallpox, and AIDS, among others.

EVOLUTION AND HOW IT HAPPENS

One look at prehistoric life, and something immediately becomes obvious: Plants and animals of the past were different from those of today. Fossils provide clues to the nature of past life. They show that species of organisms have changed many times, generation after generation, throughout the history of life. The fossil record also shows that many species have become extinct, the only clues to their existence being bones or impressions left in rock.

The species is the basic biological unit of evolution. Members of a species can interbreed and produce fertile offspring, extending the longevity of their kind and making evolution possible.

The natural process that causes species to gradually change over time is called evolution. This process is driven by changes to the genetic code—the DNA—of organisms. These genetic changes are then passed along to the next generation of a species. These changes sometimes result in dramatic changes to a species over many generations.

DNA, or deoxyribonucleic acid, is a molecule found in cells. It contains the master plan for the growth and shape of an organism. DNA contains **genes**, each of which is a section of DNA that controls one or more inherited traits. The science of genes and DNA is called genetics. When two organisms mate, each one of their offspring contains a unique combination of genes derived from the parent's DNA.

How do changes happen to a species? How do new species of life come into being? These are the same questions that tantalized the British naturalist Charles Darwin (1809–1882). The fact that offspring inherited traits from their parents had been noticed in his time, but Darwin and other scientists had no idea how this happened. They possessed no knowledge of genes and DNA. Darwin sought answers by studying animals in the natural world. In 1859, after many years of making observations in nature, he published *The Origin of Species by Means of Natural Selection*, a carefully reasoned treatise in which he explained what he had noticed about the adaptability of life. Darwin deduced all of his theories related to evolution by understanding the relationship between living organisms, their offspring, and their habitat.

Darwin's theories were based on two important observations. He saw that offspring inherit physical traits from their parents. Furthermore, offspring are never identical to their parents, and no two offspring of the same parents are identical. Each offspring includes a unique combination of characteristics inherited from its parents.

Darwin also observed that many more offspring are produced by a species than will survive long enough to reproduce on their own.

From these observations, Darwin drew two significant conclusions. First, that in our world of many diverse living things, there is an ongoing struggle for survival. Darwin wrote that "many more individuals of each species are born than can survive." Darwin saw that the variation of traits within a given species make some individuals more likely to survive. The reasons why some individuals survive and others do not led Darwin to his second conclusion. Given the complex and changing conditions under which life exists, those individuals with the most favorable combination of inherited traits may survive and reproduce while others may not. Nature is the judge and jury of which ones make the grade. For this reason, Darwin called this process natural selection, meaning that the natural laws of inheritance provide or assure, by chance, that some members of a species are better equipped for survival than others.

For example, a wild boar with stronger leg muscles might be able to outrun a lion better than a slower and weaker wild boar. Any organism that lives long enough to mature, mate, and have offspring is capable of passing along its superior traits. If the faster, stronger boar lives to reproduce, it might pass along its stronger leg muscles to its offspring. Over many generations, wild boars with this quality might continue to have a better chance of survival, thus continuing a trend toward faster and stronger wild boars. After many genera-tions and possibly thousands, even millions of years, the wild boars might become so different that they will evolve into a new species. Changes such as this have happened many times in the history of life. Evidence for natural selection can be seen clearly in the fossil record of such animals as horses, whales, and birds.

Living species represent moments in the ongoing process of evolution. There is no such thing as a species that has stopped evolving. Humans and all other species on the planet continue to change with each successive generation, even if only in ways that are nearly imperceptible. Evolution is influenced by inherited traits and changes in the environment. Knowing how these kinds of changes affected past organisms is a key to seeing the future of life.

"To know the past is to understand the present." Many people, especially scientists, use this quote as a guide and for inspiration.

IS THERE A REASON FOR EVOLUTION?

Every species possesses, by chance, genetic traits that may improve or hinder its chances of survival. Despite human scientists' success in artificially modifying genetic code, the inheritance of biological traits in nature is not under an individual organism's control. In the natural world, an organism cannot dictate which traits it will inherit, nor can its parents direct which traits to pass along. The traits are passed along by chance in the form of **mutations**—slight, unpredictable variations in the genetic code that happen when organisms reproduce.

The word *mutation* implies that something bad has happened. Mutations, however, are not always bad. They might result in larger ears, longer fingers, a slightly different colored eye, or any number of other possible changes to the biology of an organism. None of these traits, however, is guaranteed to help or hurt an individual's survival. Destructive mutations are also possible, such as brain damage, badly-formed bones, and other disabling conditions that hurt the chances of an organism to make it in the world, particularly in nature.

Evolution is the result of natural selection; and it, too, happens by chance. Evolution has no goal or direction but effectively weeds out organisms that are better fit—better designed—to survive whatever nature throws in their path. Evolution does not affect all life in the same way. Plants and animals do not necessarily evolve into bigger individuals. Nor do they always have to become stronger, louder, faster, taller or any other biologically-based trait one can think of. While being bigger and stronger might improve the likelihood of survival for some species, there are compelling examples of animals that evolved in the opposite direction, resulting in smaller species. Similarly, even though land animals originally evolved from fish, there are cases, as in the whale, where land animals have returned to an aquatic lifestyle.

The direction of evolution is set in motion first by the traits inherited by individuals and then by the interaction of that individual with its habitat. These interconnected processes are sometimes referred to as "nature and nurture." "Nature" provides the traits associated with one's genetic makeup. "Nurture" is the overall effect of the environment on an organism. If a man is six feet (1.8 m) tall, has brown eyes, and loses his hair to baldness, he has been affected by nature—his natural genetic makeup. If he loses a finger due to an accident, he will not have offspring born with a missing finger.

The idea of nurturing brings into the discussion the subjects of intelligence, behavior, and personality. Personal traits such as hobbies, interests, and mental skills are largely shaped by the environment in which a person is raised. Such circumstances are difficult to define and predict, but they can make one person an avid comic book collector, another person a fan of Shakespeare, and yet another a student of both. These are examples of individual learned behavior, personal traits that are not inherited through genes.

There is evidence, however, that social behaviors of a given species can be inherited. Such species behaviors as parental care in gibbons, foraging tactics of shore crabs, territorial behavior in African sunbirds, and pack hunting in lions are adaptive and the result of natural selection.

Evolution, then, has two causes. It is influenced by the inherited genetic traits of an individual organism *and* by the interaction of an organism with its habitat. If an organism successfully survives in its habitat long enough to mate and pass its genetic code on to its offspring, then evolution continues for that species.

ADAPTATION

Life-forms are sometimes found in the most unlikely places. No matter where one looks on Earth, life seems to have grabbed a foothold. From the highest mountains to the depths of the deepest oceans, from the wet tropics to the hot and dry deserts, there is life. How is it that organisms are able to survive in such harsh environments?

Biological traits that make an organism better fit to survive are called adaptations. If it is successfully adapted, an organism can stay alive and reproduce.

Natural selection is the mechanism behind evolution that adjusts the physiology of plants and animals over generations to cope with mutable environmental forces. Adaptations may protect a species from stressful changes to its habitat, help members of the species to avoid predators, and make the species resistant to chemicals such as pesticides. In each case, an adaptation helps an organism take advantage of an opportunity to spread and reproduce. Some of the best evidence for genetically transferred biological adaptations comes from the study of the suitability of organisms to their environments. Birds, for example, come in many species, each with its own particular physical characteristics. A trait of birds that varies widely is the size and shape of the beak. Long, pointed beaks are suited for penetrating tree bark in search of hidden insects; big beaks are suited for eating large seeds; small beaks are suited for eating small seeds; and so forth. In every known natural habitat, the size and shape of bird beaks have adapted for the size and shape of the food that each bird eats. The design of the beak is an adaptation, a physiological adjustment brought about through natural selection over a long period of time.

Adaptation within the field of evolution focuses on genetically inherited traits that are driven by natural selection. In evolution, the only adaptations that matter are those that can be passed to the next generation. This should not be confused with other forms of adaptation that affect individuals within a species population but that are not genetically based.

There are two other forms of biological adaptation in addition to inheritable adaptive traits. These are **short-term** and **long-term biological adaptations** that develop during the life of an individual but are not inheritable. Short- and long-term adaptations are "nurturing" traits acquired during an organism's life. Until the science of genetics was able to prove which kinds of biological adaptations could be inherited, there was much scientific debate about the transference of these observable traits. It is worth contrasting the three forms of biological adaptation by means of examples that make their differences clear. One need look no further than humans for these examples. The ways in which humans biologically adapt to living at high altitudes provide examples of all three forms of biological adaptation.

Living at the Top of the World: Three Kinds of Human Adaptation

The three kinds of biological adaptation can be illustrated by examining the ways that humans cope physiologically with living at mountain elevations. To understand these examples, a quick lesson about the human respiratory system is in order.

Oxygen is one of the essential elements needed by organisms. Humans get their oxygen from the air. When we breathe, our lungs extract oxygen from the air and transfer it to the blood. Once in the blood, life-giving oxygen is carried through our veins by a protein called hemoglobin. Oxygen is an essential fuel for the body's tissues. Being without oxygen for just a little while can irreparably damage sensitive tissues and organs, such as the human brain. Being totally without oxygen for three or more minutes can kill a human.

The amount of oxygen found in the air varies with elevation. At sea level, the air is most saturated with oxygen. At higher elevations, especially mountain elevations, the concentration of oxygen in the air is measurably "thinner."

Having evolved near sea level, the human body is optimally suited for breathing and functioning at low elevations where the air is richest with oxygen—from about 50 feet (more than 15 m) to about 2,000 to 4,000 feet (about 600 to 1,200 m) above sea level, for example. Most humans do not live at elevations higher than that.

The amount of oxygen in the air begins to thin out at elevations above 8,125 feet (about 2,440 m), such as air found on a mountain or highland plain. People inhale less oxygen with each breath at those elevations. Those who travel to such altitudes may experience physiological side effects. A body that is accustomed to having a certain amount of oxygen in the air will tire more quickly when the air is thinner. The situation becomes even more risky at altitudes over 10,560 feet (more than 3,000 m). At these elevations, a person will get altitude sickness, also known as hypoxia. This condition is due to low oxygen concentration in the air. Hypoxia can result in headaches, fatigue, dizziness, shortness of breath, loss of appetite, and nausea. At elevations over 25,000 feet (more than 7,600 m), the oxygen is so sparse that hypoxia will kill a person.

HUMAN ALTITUDE ADAPTATIONS

Elevation	Adaptation
At sea level to about 4,000 feet (about 1,200 m)	Most humans are optimized to live at sea level
Between 4,000 and 8,000 feet (about 1,200 to 2,440 m)	Short-term and long-term biological adaptation takes place
Above 8,000 feet (about 2,440 m)	Some human populations have adapted permanent biological adaptations to fend off hypoxia.

Hypoxia may seem like a biological imperative; yet, given enough time to adjust, humans can adapt their bodies to cope with dangerously thin air. People have three different kinds of biological adaptations to higher altitudes and thinner air.

The first kind of biological adaptation occurs when a person is new to the mountains. He or she will experience a short-term physiological adaptation, that might include shortness of breath and a rapid heartbeat as the body adjusts to the thinner air. By breathing more rapidly, a person can inhale an amount of air comparable to that taken in by longer, slower breaths during the same amount of time. When the person's heart beats faster, it compensates for less oxygen in the air by pumping the oxygen that *is* available more rapidly, thus fueling tissues and organs at acceptable rates. Rapid breathing and an accelerated heart rate are both ways that the body automatically adjusts to a lower amount of breathable oxygen.

A person born in a lowland area who grows up in a higher altitude region, or even a person who moves to a higher altitude as an adult, may experience the second kind of biological adaptation, a long-term physiological change that occurs as the person acclimates to the environment. Such a person's lungs and circulatory system can become more efficient at taking oxygen from thin air. The person may develop more red blood cells and vessels to carry oxygen, the person's lungs may grow larger to improve oxygen exchange, and the muscles of the person's respiratory and vascular systems may become stronger to accommodate the processing of oxygen under these more stressful conditions. These changes, however, are for the individual only; they cannot be passed on genetically.

The third kind of biological adaptation is a genetic one that is transferred from one generation to the next through DNA. A group of native peoples that has lived in a mountainous region for many generations might inherit genetic advantages for living at high altitudes. Three excellent examples of this have been documented in populations dwelling in mountains in different parts of the world. Most surprisingly, each of these groups has evolved a different biological adaptation for coping with thin air.

Tourists visiting the highland plains of Tibet in Central Asia, the Andes Mountains in South America, or the highlands of Ethiopia in Africa soon find themselves gasping for air. It is astounding to visitors to these regions that the rugged residents, who live at elevations greater than 11,000 feet (about 3,300 m), can go about their daily chores without losing their breath. They conduct their daily business unhindered by the fact that they live at an altitude where the air has only two-thirds as much oxygen as at sea level. Each of these populations has developed its own unique physiological immunity to hypoxia.

The Andeans battle the thin air by having developed higher concentrations of oxygen-carrying hemoglobin in their blood. The Andeans' lungs can grab more oxygen from the air with each breath, effectively counteracting the potential effects of hypoxia.

The Tibetans cope with thin air in a much different way. First, they breathe faster than people living at sea level. By taking in more breaths per minute, they can inhale more oxygen. Unlike the Andeans, however, the blood of the Tibetans does not have more hemoglobin than normal. To compensate for the low oxygen content of their blood, the Tibetans have wider blood vessels—wider tubes to carry blood to their bodies' tissues. Having wider vessels increases the amount of blood and oxygen that reaches the tissues with each beat of the heart.

The Andeans and Tibetans are examples of organisms with genetically based biological adaptations. These adaptations can be passed along to offspring and probably become slightly more efficient with each successive generation. Biological adaptations clearly take a long period, and many generations, to develop. To consider these two peoples historically, the Tibetans are the older, having first populated their mountains about 23,000 years ago. The Andeans have been in their mountains for about 10,000 years.

There is yet a third example, in Ethiopia, of a highland population that has adapted amazingly well to mountainous living. Despite the fact that they live at an elevation of about 11,580 feet (about 3,530 m), a zone where hypoxia should be in effect, these people also show no signs of altitude sickness. Most puzzling, though, is that the highland people of Ethiopia do not have either of the biological adaptations of the Tibetans and Andeans. In fact, the proportion of hemoglobin in the Ethiopians' blood is about the same as that of people living at sea level. The mechanism of their biological adaptation remains a mystery. It is also worth noting that the Ethiopians have been native to their mountains for about 50,000 years—twice as long as the Tibetans and five times longer than the Andeans. The Ethiopians evidently represent a third form of evolutionary adaptation to highland living that is genetically passed along to each generation. Scientists, however, have yet to decipher the biological basis for the Ethiopians' remarkable robustness for mountain living.

The following table shows three ways that humans adapt biologically to their environment.

FORMS OF BIOLOGICAL ADAPTATION

Type of Adaptation	Cause	Example
Short-term physiological change	Occurs naturally when an organism encounters a change to its environment	Person experiences faster heart rate and takes gulps of air (hyperventilation)
Long-term physiological change	Occurs during the growth stage of an individual organism or during long-term exposure to a new or changing environment	Respiratory system becomes better at extracting oxygen from thin air
Genetic change	Occurs over many generations	Larger chest cavity of native highlanders absorbs more oxygen from thin air

In addition to the three forms of biological adaptation, humans have the unique ability to make additional adaptations using technology. Clothing is one simple but effective technology humans use to adapt to different climates. Mountain climbers inhale oxygen from oxygen tanks to compensate for the lower levels of oxygen at high altitudes. Other technological adaptations are dazzling, such as spacecraft, submarines, and other portable environments humans have created to protect human life in places where it cannot survive without help.

THE RATE OF EVOLUTION

Darwin viewed evolution and the emergence of new species as a slow and gradual process. In his view, it took thousands or even millions of years to create a new species. This view is called **gradualism**. Gradualism means that slow and gradual changes over a long period of time lead to major biological changes to a species. The gradual development of a new species begins with mutations and is then magnified or isolated by natural selection. The fossil record does indeed provide many clues to such gradual changes.

The concept of gradualism was challenged in 1972 by a bold new idea proposed by paleontologists Stephen Jay Gould (1941–2002) and Niles Eldredge (b. 1943). Gould and Eldredge still assumed that natural selection was the underlying machinery of evolution, but they noticed that evolution does not always occur at a slow and gradual pace. The fossil record shows that many species can go for millions of years without any significant changes. It is as if evolution were standing still for some species. Living examples such as the cockroach and a fish called the bowfin seem to follow this pattern, having not changed significantly for many millions of years. This can change, however, if a population of a given species suddenly encounters a dramatic change to its habitat. This might be caused by a geological event, a change in climate, or perhaps even interaction with other species. Following such occurrences, a short period of rapid evolution may take place that affects a subset of a species population. Those members of a species population with certain traits that favor their survival may change dramatically over a period of tens of thousands or several million years—mere seconds and minutes on the scale of geologic time. The changes may result in new species. This rapid twist to the evolutionary story is called **punctuated equilibria**.

Evolution is typically thought of as a linear process in which a given species gradually evolves into another due to a barrier to its continued existence, such as a geographic change. This path to a new species is called allopatric speciation. In this case, a given species population is affected by a barrier (such as mountain formation) and the divided groups evolve in isolation from one another. If the separated populations are subjected to dissimilar adaptive pressures, a new species may result.

In contrast to allopatric speciation, it is possible for a new species to emerge from within a parent population even while occupying the same geographic space. This splitting of lineages is rarer than allopatric speciation but has been observed in a variety of plants and animals, including insects that become dependent on different kinds of plants even though they live in the same range.

The evidence for rapid evolution is usually found in a small portion of an overall species population. For example, when insects are exposed to pesticides, certain members of the population can rapidly develop resistance. The same can be said of bacteria that grow resistant to antibiotic medicines. These adaptations are the result of natural selection. Such changes can mark the beginning of the development of a new species.

The fossil record of the flowering plants provides a dramatic example of evolutionary opportunism and the influence of one species of life on another. All plants, including flowering plants, reproduce using pollinization, the physical transmittal of a plant's "male" pollen to a plant's "female" seed. In flowering plants, pollinization is aided by the interaction of insects or birds that transport pollen when they come in contact with a plant. The earliest fossil evidence of the leaves of flowering plants shows that they were simple in shape and had poorly organized veins. The earliest examples of pollen were also primitive, with an unadorned surface structure. As time went on, both leaves and pollen evolved more complex structures that aided their survival. Leaf structures became broader and varied in shape, with geometrically laid-out veins, features that added to the robustness of the plants. Pollen began to exhibit a more sculpted surface texture that was more easily grabbed by insects and birds that transported the pollen to facilitate pollination. Colorful flowers also evolved, enhancing the attraction of a plant to insects and birds. The quick ascent of flowering plants to their position as the most populous of all plants took about 10 million years. This spectacular rise was due to the co-evolving and mutually beneficial relationship between flowering plants and the birds and insects that facilitated their pollination.

What can be concluded from this is that the rate of evolution for any given species will vary depending on the biologic, geographic, and environmental circumstances affecting a population of organisms. Evolution may be slow and gradual, as Darwin thought, or rapid, as Gould and Eldredge suggested. The facts favor a wide range of evolutionary rates on a spectrum represented by gradualism at one end and punctuated equilibria at the other.

EVIDENCE FOR EVOLUTION

Evolution begins with the assumption that life has existed for billions of years and changes continually over time. Evolution takes place at a fairly rapid rate when compared to the billions of years of Earth's geologic history. To humans, however, these changes are so slow as to go unnoticed. If evolution is such a slow process, how can it be proved? Evidence for evolution comes from three lines of investigation: examining the fossil record, studying biological molecules and genes, and the field of comparative anatomy.

Evidence from the Fossil Record

Soon after Darwin published his theories in 1859, other scientists began to look for evidence of evolution in the fossil record. Only two years later, in 1861, a most amazing fossil was uncovered in the Bavarian region of Germany. Preserved as a flattened-out specimen in fine-grained limestone deposits, the small creature resembled both a small reptilian dinosaur and a feathered bird. Dating from 145 million years ago, it was, in fact, the oldest known bird, *Archaeopteryx* ("ancient wing"). Unlike birds of today, it had teeth and a tail, much like a small meat-eating dinosaur. Finely etched markings around the skeleton also revealed impressions of wing feathers. *Archaeopteryx* was a remarkable transition between dinosaurs, which came first, and birds. It is now widely believed that birds are the living descendents of small, bipedal dinosaurs similar to *Compsognathus*. *Archaeopteryx* represented a transition stage in evolution from a ground-dwelling creature to a flying creature.

Archaeopteryx is an example of a **transitional fossil.** A transitional fossil shows just one step in the many stages that exist as species evolve. Sometimes transitional fossils are found for closely related species; at other times, transitional fossils are found for

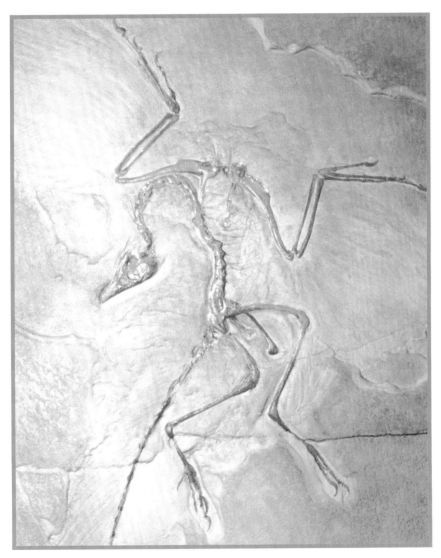

Archaeopteryx, the first-known bird, is a transitional fossil showing traits found in dinosaurs and birds.

families of organisms that are less directly related. In the case of *Archaeopteryx*, no other fossils of its relatives dating from just before or after its appearance have yet been found, so other stages in the development of *Archaeopteryx* are currently unknown. Recent findings in northeast China, however, in younger fossil beds dating from 125 million years ago, have provided many examples of transitional forms between dinosaurs and birds. These Chinese fossils are not directly related to *Archaeopteryx*, but they suggest the kinds of evolutionary changes that also may have been taking place in Germany, where the official "first bird" was discovered.

Transitional fossils can provide powerful evidence for evolution. A dramatic example is that of the evolution of early whales. *Pakicetus* was an early ancestor to the modern whale. This creature lived about 50 million years ago. A fossil of its skull shows that its nostrils were at the front of its long skull. A modern beluga whale has a skull with many similarities to *Pakicetus,* but its nostrils are on top of its skull. This suggests that over time, as species of whales evolved, the nostrils gradually moved to the top of the skull. A paleontologist looking for a transitional form in the evolution of the whale would expect to find a fossil with the nostrils located somewhere in between those of *Pakicetus* and those of the beluga whale. That transitional form exists in the skull of *Aetiocetus*, a whale ancestor from 25 million years ago that has its nostrils midway between the end of its nose and the top of its skull.

The fossil record for the evolution of the modern horse from its most distant ancestors is full of gaps. Paleontologists do not know all of the steps that led from the pig-sized horse ancestors that lived 55 million years ago to the modern stallion. Enough fossils have been found of distantly related horse relatives, however, to reveal a remarkable record of transition. The front foot of the horse did not always have just one toe, or hoof, as it does today. The horse's earliest ancestors had four toes. Over millions of years, the environment of horse ancestors changed, from a tropical woodland to a vast open plain with grasses. The ability to run fast to escape predators became more and more vital to the survival of ancient horses. The

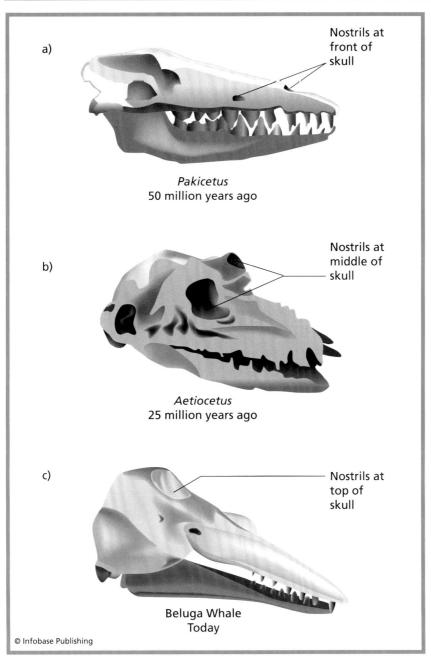

a)

Nostrils at
front of
skull

Pakicetus
50 million years ago

b)

Nostrils at
middle of
skull

Aetiocetus
25 million years ago

c)

Nostrils at
top of
skull

Beluga Whale
Today

© Infobase Publishing

This transitional sequence in the evolution of the beluga whale shows how
the nostrils moved from the front of the skull to the top of the skull over
several million years.

feet of ancient horses gradually favored fewer and fewer toes. The fossil record includes horses with three, two, and finally one toe on each foot. With each transition, the third toe of the foot became increasingly bigger than the other, providing superior footing. This led to the sure-footed single hoof of the modern horse, one of the fastest animals alive.

Many more dramatic examples of transitional fossils exist, documenting the evolution of invertebrates, plants, sharks and other fish, amphibians, reptiles, mammals, and birds. Fossils are like photographs that capture a moment in evolution, thereby allowing us to see what was happening in the lineage of a species.

Evidence from Biological Molecules and Genes

Since the discovery in the 1950s that the DNA molecule carried genetic traits, molecular biologists have made great strides in decoding the DNA of many kinds of organisms. Although the mysteries of DNA are far from solved, what has been learned from DNA reinforces the fact that evolution happens.

One startling fact is that the DNA of all organisms is composed of the same set of 20 amino acids. This fact alone strongly suggests that all organisms—conifers and clams, dachshunds and daffodils—are descended from one common ancestor. This common ancestor may have been a single-celled organism that first appeared 3.5 billion years ago. As it evolved into new species, and those species in turn continued to evolve into the whole array of life that is before us, each organism continued to carry the same basic stuff of life in its DNA molecules.

Tens of thousands of genes make up the DNA sequences of individual species. Genetic mutations occur randomly to a species over time. These mutations may be passed along to offspring and continued in future generations of a species. In this way, the original DNA sequence found in a species gradually changes over time. The DNA sequence, however, does not change so dramatically that it is no longer recognizable. Organisms that are closely related, even over enormous periods of geologic time, will still have similar DNA sequences.

Structure of DNA

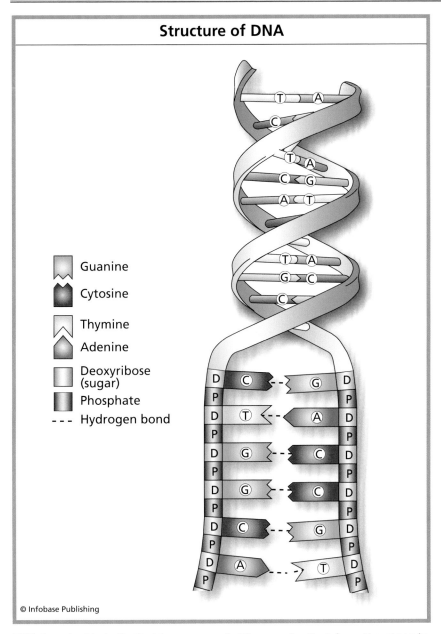

Guanine

Cytosine

Thymine

Adenine

Deoxyribose (sugar)

Phosphate

- - - Hydrogen bond

© Infobase Publishing

DNA is a double-helix that is composed of base pairs that form the steps in a ladder-like formation.

To an observer relying on physical appearances only, most creatures appear to be quite different. A starfish is not a spider monkey, and a finch is not a ferret. Sometimes, however, DNA can reveal a kinship that was not otherwise obvious. In the case of whales, for instance, it has been suggested for many years that these oceangoing mammals evolved from land creatures. Until the availability of DNA analysis, the only evidence for this theory came from the fossil record. The example of the *Pakicetus* skull is worth bringing up again. *Pakicetus* was one of the first whales. The design of its inner ear was not yet fully compatible with water life. It can be assumed that *Pakicetus* probably spent most of its time on land. *Pakicetus* was descended from a line of land-bound mammals, but which ones? DNA analysis of whales now reveals that they are most closely related to a branch of mammals that also led to the hippopotamus.

Molecular biology, then, adds further hard evidence for the phenomenon of evolution. As scientists continue to examine and compare the DNA of different living things, it may be possible to construct a tree of life that accurately shows who is related to whom. Such a tree will probably debunk many long-held assumptions about the family tree of animals alive today.

This naturally leads the curious mind to ask, what about the DNA of extinct creatures? Is it possible to extract DNA from a fossil bone? The answer is a qualified yes. The older the fossil, however, the less likely it is that DNA can be extracted from it. How old is old? In 1997, DNA was successfully obtained from a 40,000-year-old fossil bone of a Neandertal human. Claims have also been made of DNA being recovered from 17 million-year-old fossil leaves and 25 million-year-old fossil insects, but these results have been disputed by scientists who have been unable to reproduce the results. Indisputable pieces of fossil DNA have not yet been found in fossils as old as the dinosaurs (c. 65 million years or older), but some remnants of organic molecules sometimes become fossilized. The oldest fossils from which DNA has been recovered date from about 50,000 years ago.

Evidence From Comparative Anatomy

Further clues that evolution happens comes from the comparison of the structures of different organisms. The theory of evolution predicts that descendants will share similarities with common ancestors. Every organism has anatomical and biochemical structures that can be compared to others. **Homologies** are traits, both structural and behavioral, that different species of organisms have inherited from a common ancestor. Homologies are the basis for knowledge of how organisms are related. Homologies show which organisms evolved from which ancestors. The often sketchy similarities observed in anatomical structures can be reinforced by DNA analysis of related organisms. In the case of humans, gorillas, and chimpanzees, even though they share vague skeletal similarities, the true closeness of these species is revealed by comparing their DNA. Humans, gorillas, and chimpanzees share 98 percent of their DNA. This homology illustrates that all three descended from a common line prior to the appearance of human, gorilla, and chimpanzee species. This common descent occurred sometime before about 10 million years ago, the time after which the species of early humans, gorillas, and chimpanzees began to develop separately.

Some homologies reach back even further in time. The history of land vertebrates begins around 370 million years ago in the Late Devonian Period. Some lobe-finned fishes developed specialized front fins to support their body weight in shallow water. From this lineage came true limbed animals, including the first walking fishes whose front fins evolved into forelimbs. Beginning with this remarkable adaptation, the forelimb of vertebrates with legs (**tetrapods**) has evolved in many different ways to serve different species. No matter what their size, lifestyle, habitat, or geologic time, all tetrapods have the same set of bones in their forelimbs: the humerus, radius, and ulna. These bones are seen in tetrapods living today and in prehistoric animals. The exact shape and size of the bones may vary depending on the design of the tetrapod body, but the similarity of their forelimbs suggests that all tetrapods have a common ancestor. The history of the forelimb is another good example of a homology.

Homologies relate not only to the hard parts of an organism—the bones, teeth, shells, and other parts that become fossilized—but also

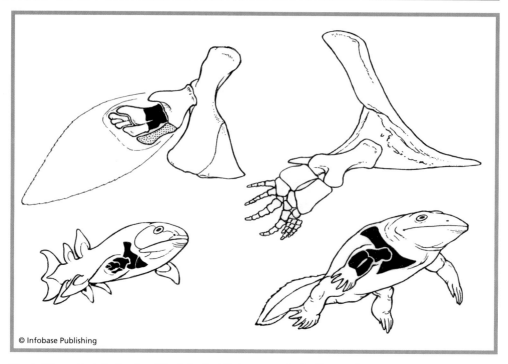

No matter what their size, lifestyle, habitat, or geologic time, all tetrapods have the same set of bones in their forelimbs. These bones are seen in tetrapods living today as well as in prehistoric animals.

to the soft tissues or organs that are not found in the fossil record, such as the heart, lungs, brain, and gut. A scientist who is given only the fossil skeleton of an extinct vertebrate can assume that that organism shared most of the internal organs of today's vertebrates. Knowing that homologies exist allows paleontologists to piece together the lifestyle of an extinct animal with some confidence.

There is an old saying, "If it looks like a duck, walks like a duck, and quacks like a duck, it must be a duck." This may be true of ducks, but it is not always true in what one sees in the fossil record.

Similar inherited traits can arise in organisms that are not related to one another. These traits are called **analogies** and are the result of **convergent evolution**. When is a duck not a duck? When it is the result of convergent evolution. Different species can sometimes respond to forces of nature in similar ways. Convergent evolution occurs when unrelated species each develop similar adaptations to similar environmental conditions.

Consider the case of powered flight. This ability is not unique to birds. Among vertebrates, powered flight has evolved at least three separate times. These instances were separated by long stretches of time and happened independently of one another. Flight in the vertebrates first happened in winged reptiles called pterosaurs, then in birds, and finally in bats, which are mammals. In each case, the forelimbs of the species changed over time to form wings. This is an example of convergent evolution. These individual species evolved powered flight at widely divergent times and places in Earth's history. Another striking case of convergent evolution involves animals of the sea. Most fishes have streamlined bodies with fins, and ocean mammals such as the porpoise have developed similar bodies with fins. Even more striking is the comparison of porpoises with ichthyosaurs, a group of extinct ocean reptiles. They are not related, even though both exhibit nearly identical body plans with hairless, scaleless bodies and flippers designed to improve locomotion through the water.

These examples of homology and analogy, convergent evolution, and inherited traits are all forms of comparative anatomy. This shows that clues to evolution can be found by studying the structures of living organisms and how they compare to extinct life-forms.

CONSTANTLY CHANGING LIFE

Erwin Schrodinger (1887–1961), a German physicist who was interested in the underlying causes of evolution, fittingly characterized the life of an individual organism as "but a minute blow of the chisel at the ever unfinished statue." For evolution is a work in progress, and the organisms that exist today are only the leading indicators of what is yet to come and what has gone before.

Many people believe that there are no more profound questions than those about the nature and development of life. Darwin's mechanism of natural selection has proved to be a durable explanation for the ways species change over time. Ample support for evolution comes from several disciplines as distinct as molecular biology, paleontology, mathematics, and quantum physics. The evidence converges on a stark realization about the nature of life. All species participate in a process called evolution that never ends. What is happening today in the cells and genetic architecture of every living organism may influence, in a small part, the continued development of that organism's species. While the study of evolution provides some answers to those profound questions about where life comes from, it has also greatly influenced the way that humans view, understand, and classify other organisms in the world. It is only through evolution that the many branches of Earth's family tree can be traced and linked from the first single-celled organisms that sprouted 3.5 billion years ago. The next chapter will explore the way that life is classified and lay the groundwork for defining organisms.

SUMMARY

This chapter explored the basic characteristics of life and the process of evolution that continues to help life adapt to changing conditions.

1. Living things are defined as having the following five traits: they are composed of one or more cells; they have a metabolism; they respond to stimuli; they are biologically stable; they can reproduce.

2. There are three domains of organisms: Bacteria (prokaryotes); Archaea (prokaryotes); and Eukarya (eukaryotes). There are six kingdoms of life-forms within the three domains, including Archaebacteria within the domain archaea; Bacteria, the only member of the domain Bacteria; and the protista, fungi, plantae, and animalia, all within the domain Eukarya.

3. By definition, viruses are not living things. Viruses are not made of cells. They are fragments of genetic material that become activated and reproduce when they come into contact with the cell of another organism.

4. Evolutionary theory is based on two important observations made by Charles Darwin. First, offspring inherit physical traits from their parents, with each offspring including a

unique combination of characteristics inherited from its parents. Second, many more offspring are produced by a species than will survive long enough to reproduce on their own.

5. Darwin suggested two important principles of evolution. First, in our world of many diverse living things, there is an ongoing struggle for survival. Second, those individuals with the most favorable combination of inherited traits may survive and reproduce while others may not. Nature is the judge and jury of which individuals make the grade. Darwin called this process natural selection, meaning that the natural laws of inheritance provide or assure, by chance, some members of a species to be better equipped for survival than others.

6. Evolution is the natural process that causes life gradually to change biologically over time.

7. Evolutionary changes to a species are caused by changes to the genetic code—the DNA—of organisms that are passed along to the next generation of a species through the process of natural selection.

8. Genetic traits are passed along by chance in the form of mutations—slight, unpredictable variations in the genetic code that happen when organisms reproduce. Physical traits and social behavior of a species can be passed along to the next generation by genes.

9. Evolution has two causes. It is influenced by the inherited genetic traits of an individual organism and by the interaction of an organism with its habitat.

10. Adaptations are biological traits that make an organism better fit to survive.

11. Evolution may occur gradually or rapidly.

12. Evidence for evolution can be found in the fossil record, the study of biological molecules and genes, and comparative anatomy.

13. Convergent evolution occurs when unrelated species each develop similar adaptations to similar environmental conditions.

6

HOW LIFE IS CLASSIFIED

The diversity of life is startling. Organisms ranging in size from single cells to giant redwood trees occupy an equally wide range of Earth habitats. This is both a joy and a bane to anyone who seeks a greater understanding of life and the relationships between organisms. Finding a reliable system for classifying life has occupied nearly 1,000 years of scientific thought.

The first ideas about the origins of and connections between organisms were based on casual observation. Observation alone, however, without any rules for organizing what is seen, does not necessarily lead to accurate knowledge about the nature of life. For centuries, there were many misconceptions and myths about the origins and relationships of animals. The Romans thought that the giraffe was the offspring of a camel and a leopard, and they called it the camelopard. That idea, however ingenious, violates what is known today to be the immutable reproductive boundaries between species. In Scandinavian legend, a notoriously gluttonous creature called the *gulon* was thought to be a cross between several different mammals. It had the shaggy hair of a dog, the face and claws of a cat, and the tail of a fox. Descriptions of the gulon are now thought to have originated in attempts to describe the common wolverine.

This chapter introduces the subject of the scientific classification of life, a discipline that has grown immensely since the initial work of Carolus Linnaeus in the eighteenth century. Understanding how organisms are related is a key to finding their ancestral relationships in the fossil record. Knowing the prehistory of an organism reveals ways in which life has adapted to the constantly changing Earth and its ecosystems.

The science of classifying living species and extinct species of organisms is called **taxonomy,** a word that comes from Greek roots meaning "arranging rules." A **taxon** is a single kind of organism; the plural of taxon, **taxa,** is used to describe a group of related organisms. Biologists and paleontologists are trained in the taxonomy of living organisms and fossil organisms.

EARLY CLASSIFICATION METHODS

The first scholars to classify organisms began by looking closely at organisms and found similarities and differences in their body forms. The observation of such shared characteristics led scholars to group together organisms that were similar in some ways. The Greek philosopher Aristotle was the first to place all organisms into one of two great kingdoms, the plants and the animals. Other Greek and Roman philosophers extended Aristotle's system by further dividing plants and animals into subgroups. They based such groupings on the physical similarities of organisms, such as size, parts, and shape. The Greeks and Romans recognized groups such as cats, dogs, horses, and various kinds of trees. This approach to identifying plants and animals worked for several hundred years, but the lists of organisms and their groups grew very long.

A more effective and informative approach to naming and grouping organisms was invented by the Swedish botanist Carolus Linnaeus. With the publication of his groundbreaking work *Systema Naturae* in 1758, Linnaeus suggested that nature could be further organized into a grand hierarchy of groups within groups. The great botanist recognized a species as the most basic biological unit of life, and he grouped species within ever-widening categories of organisms based on the similarities of their structures. By choosing the species as his basic building block for classification, Linnaeus was the first scientist to establish a rule that reflected a true comprehension of the way nature works. Now it could be seen at once why such early speculative misconceptions as the camelopard and the gulon could no longer be considered valid: Species cannot interbreed. Furthermore, Linnaeus used close observation to categorize his species within ever-widening groups of related organisms. The dog, for example, is part of a group—the carnivora, or meat eaters—that also includes such diverse animals as cats, bears, pandas, weasels, sea lions, walruses, and others. The carnivora, in turn, are part of a larger group, the mammals. Mammals, in turn, are grouped with other animals with backbones, the vertebrates, including fish, amphibians, reptiles, and birds. The vertebrates are then grouped with all animals without backbones to form the kingdom of animals. This nested hierarchy of groups was widely accepted and refined for more than 200 years. The branching structure of the Linnaean system also lent itself nicely to a visual representation in the form of a family tree of life. Using the method devised by Linnaeus, all life could be classified using seven categories: kingdom, phylum, class, order, family, genus, and species.

LINNAEAN CLASSIFICATION OF HUMANS

The table below shows where humans fit within the Linnaean classification of organisms.

Linnaean Category	Name of Category in the Classification of Humans	What the Category Includes
Kingdom	Animalia	All living and extinct animals
Phylum	Chordata	Animals having a backbone (vertebrates)
Class	Mammalia	Warm-blooded vertebrates, the females of which have mammary glands
Order	Primates	Living and extinct monkeys, apes, and prosimians, including humans
Super Family	Hominoidea	Living and extinct apes and humans
Family	Hominidae	Living and extinct great apes
Genus	*Homo*	Living and extinct humans
Species	*Homo sapiens**	Modern humans

*Note: The species names always consists of two parts—the genus name followed by the species name, both printed in italics.

Linnaeus also established the binomial naming system still used to give organisms their scientific names. Taxonomists around the world agree that no two organisms can have the same scientific name, and a rigorous system is in place to nominate and approve all names. The scientific name is in Latin to ensure that scientists of every nationality use the same name. At the species level of the taxonomic hierarchy, the name is "binomial" and consists of two parts. (The word *binomial* comes from Latin and means "having two parts."). The first part of the name is the genus to which the organism belongs. The second part of the name is that of the individual species. For example, the scientific name of the honeybee is *Apis mellifera.*

The Linnaean classification system, although revolutionary in its time, was limited by the extent of eighteenth-century scientific knowledge. Linnaean taxonomy was disciplined and rigorous but was based solely on identifying homologies with the naked eye. Scholars using it did not have the benefits of molecular biology and genetic science to help them understand how DNA and inherited traits affect the relationships of species. In addition, the concept of a "past" or extinct species was not widely accepted until nearly 100 years after the publication of *Systema Naturae.* Because fossils were not understood to be the remnants of ancient life that no longer existed, the fossil record was not used by Linnaeus and his followers to link living and past species. This left unrecognized the great antiquity of ancestral life and the relationship of past and present species. The result was a bulky tree of life with many more groups of organisms than were needed and no branches that ever stopped growing. The Linnaean tree of life was in need of a good pruning.

MODERN CLASSIFICATION METHODS

Like Linnaean classification, modern taxonomy is based on finding homologies—the same features, found in different species. Unlike Linnaean classification, however, the tools available to today's scientists help those scientists to reach far beyond what can be seen with the naked eye. This has led to significant refinements in the classification of life.

The modern classification of organisms is based on the broad analysis of organisms in the laboratory or in the field with respect to individual members of a species, populations, communities, and entire ecosystems. The modern view of what makes up a species is now informed by many disciplines in science. As biologist Lynn

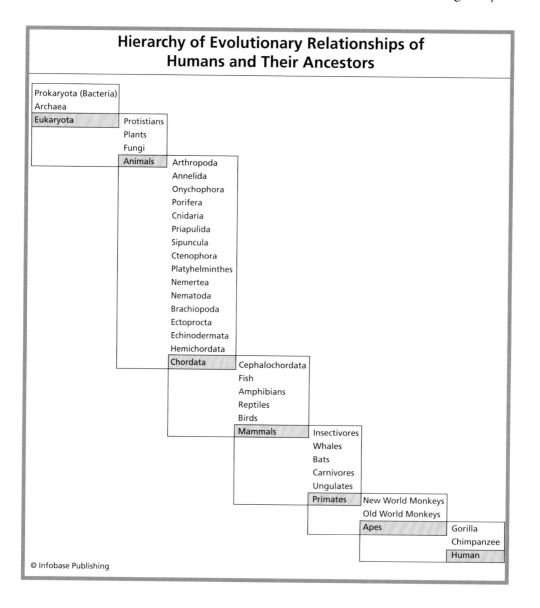

Margulis explains, "Organisms are classified—on the basis of body form, genetic similarity, metabolism (body chemistry), developmental pattern, behavior, and (in principle) all their characteristics—together with similar organisms in a group called a species." By considering all of these factors, taxonomists can use homologies to help establish evolutionary relationships between species. For example, the leg of a horse and the flipper of a dolphin are homologous because they are evolved from the same bone in an ancestor common to both of them. A history of the evolutionary relationships among species is called a **phylogeny.**

Whereas Linnaean classification was based only on analyzing the physical characteristics of an organism that could be seen with the naked eye, modern taxonomic methods recognize that traits can be morphological or molecular. Two different but complementary practices are currently used for classifying organisms. The first is **cladistics**, an analytical technique that compares the morphological features of species, such as their skeletons. In cladistics, organisms are grouped because of their

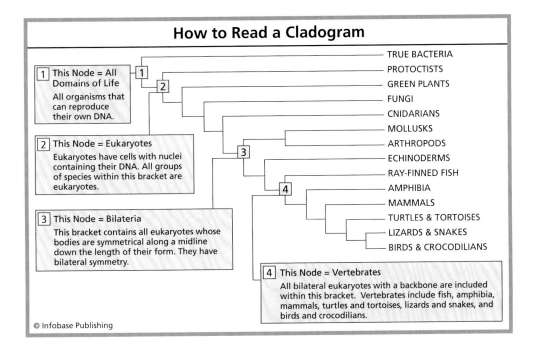

How to Read a Cladogram

TRUE BACTERIA
PROTOCTISTS
GREEN PLANTS
FUNGI
CNIDARIANS
MOLLUSKS
ARTHROPODS
ECHINODERMS
RAY-FINNED FISH
AMPHIBIA
MAMMALS
TURTLES & TORTOISES
LIZARDS & SNAKES
BIRDS & CROCODILIANS

1 This Node = All Domains of Life
All organisms that can reproduce their own DNA.

2 This Node = Eukaryotes
Eukaryotes have cells with nuclei containing their DNA. All groups of species within this bracket are eukaryotes.

3 This Node = Bilateria
This bracket contains all eukaryotes whose bodies are symmetrical along a midline down the length of their form. They have bilateral symmetry.

4 This Node = Vertebrates
All bilateral eukaryotes with a backbone are included within this bracket. Vertebrates include fish, amphibia, mammals, turtles and tortoises, lizards and snakes, and birds and crocodilians.

shared characteristics. These shared characteristics confirm the evolutionary links that bind different species into related groups. These relationships can be illustrated for a related group using a diagram called a **cladogram.**

The second technique for classifying organisms and confirming evolutionary relationships is called **molecular cladistics.** This discipline compares biological elements of different species at the molecular level and includes the study of genes and DNA. When used with morphological cladistics, molecular evidence can verify and clarify evolutionary relationships that are not obvious in a comparison of anatomical features only.

Both of these techniques can be used to verify the taxonomy of living and extinct species. In the case of living organisms, scientists wishing to compare anatomical and genetic traits have ready access to living specimens. The taxonomic study of fossil organisms can be trickier. Given enough well-preserved fossil specimens of a given species, scientists can use that species' morphological features to produce a comprehensive cladistic analysis. For example, there are several members of the family Tyrannosauroidea, the largest predatory dinosaurs that roamed North America and Asia during the Late Cretaceous Period. Among these dinosaurs is the genus *Tyrannosaurus*, but there are several others, including *Albertosaurus*, *Daspletosaurus*, *Gorgosaurus*, and *Tarbosaurus*. The differences between these genera of tyrannosaurs have been defined using morphological analysis. Factors making them cladistically distinct from one another include the size of the skull, the size and shape of the teeth, the position and shape of the eyes, the nasal bones, and many other diagnostically comparable features.

Applying molecular cladistics to fossil specimens is not as easy as comparing their bones. Scientists cannot reliably obtain traces of organic molecules, such as blood, of any kind from specimens that are older than 100,000 years. DNA is even tougher to obtain from a fossil and generally isn't found intact in specimens older than 50,000 years. There have been recent exceptions to these rules of thumb, however. In March 2005, paleontologist Mary Schweitzer announced the discovery of preserved leg tissue in the fossil of a 68 million-year-old *Tyrannosaurus*, possibly containing blood vessels and cells. This may allow Schweitzer to analyze fragmentary DNA molecules, but nothing on the scale of the cloning of dinosaurs as described in *Jurassic Park* is even remotely possible with present technology. Even the most fragmentary bits of organic molecules and DNA can sometimes be used by scientists to unlock the mysteries of evolutionary relationships among species, however. The use of molecular cladistics to help classify fossil organisms is a promising, growing part of taxonomic analysis.

Combining data about living organisms with evidence from the fossil record allows a paleontologist to understand the evolution of species over a long period of time. This makes it possible to diagram a phylogenetic tree of life showing the evolution of organisms over millions of years.

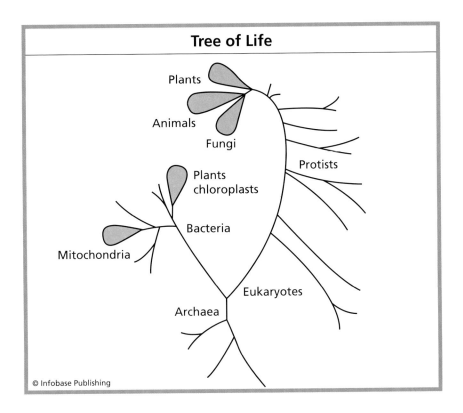

© Infobase Publishing

The use of computers also has revolutionized the field of taxonomy. In cladistics, with computers, a scientist can analyze quickly large amounts of comparative data about fossil specimens to show how they might be related. Special software can draw a cladogram for a paleontologist who enters the many data needed to analyze and compare a set of specimens.

Computers are also important to the analysis of DNA molecules. To understand how DNA works, scientists need to understand how it is put together. Human DNA is found in 24 different chromosomes and is made up of 3 billion chemical building blocks. Without the aid of computers, it would be virtually impossible for people to map the sequence of these building blocks to understand how human DNA is put together. The same can be said for any other organism: The organization of the tremendous number of elements that make up DNA can be understood only with the help of a computer.

Scientists, however, do not use computers only to help them understand the DNA of living organisms. Recently, scientists have begun using computers to reconstruct the likely gene sequences of extinct organisms. Because intact DNA cannot be reliably obtained from fossils that are more than 50,000 years old, some innovative scientists have turned to computers to help them decipher the evolution of species. One such case is a team led by computer scientist Mathieu Blanchette that created software to analyze the known DNA of living animals, which then could be worked backward to assemble the likely DNA sequences of their extinct ancestors. In one experiment, the scientists began with the DNA of 19 different living mammals, including a pig, a human, and a rat, to try to define a DNA sequence for their common ancestor, believed by paleontologists to be a small, shrewlike animal that lived over 70 million years ago. The software created a possible DNA sequence for this distant ancestor. This computer work also provided clues as to when various new species of mammals may have branched off from their humble beginnings. Computer software that can reconstruct possible DNA sequences for extinct animals will enable scientists to create a more complete picture of evolution by filling-in gaps in the fossil record.

CLASSIFICATION LEADS TO GREATER UNDERSTANDING

In the 250 years since Linnaeus introduced his classification system, science has greatly broadened its knowledge of species of all kinds. By 1758, Linnaeus had classified about 12,100 plant and animal species, a stupendous feat for one individual. His pioneering work was the cornerstone for the classification of species that would follow. Today, with the inclusion of fossil species, scientists recognize about 1.75 million species of life, and many more are added each year. Current estimates as to the total number of living species range from 3 million to 30 million, with some of the most frequently discovered species being among the archaebacteria.

One of the first steps toward better understanding the world is to label and categorize the things that are found in it. Classifying things reveals relationships between organisms but can also portray the adaptation and evolution of life as part of the bigger picture of the Earth and its ecosystems.

SUMMARY

This chapter introduced the subject of the scientific classification of life.

1. The science of classifying living and extinct species is called taxonomy. A taxon is a group of related organisms.
2. Swedish botanist Carolus Linnaeus (1707–1778) introduced a plan for classifying all plant and animal life and the binomial system for giving organisms their scientific names.
3. Linnaeus based his classification on the observable physical characteristics of organisms. He used the species as the most basic biological unit of his hierarchy.
4. Using the Linnaean hierarchical classification system, all life could be classified using seven categories: kingdom, phylum, class, order, family, genus, and species.
5. A history of the evolutionary relationships among species is called a phylogeny.

6. Whereas Linnaean classification was based only on analysis of the physical characteristics of an organism that could be seen with the naked eye, modern taxonomic methods recognize that traits can be morphological or molecular.

7. Cladistics is a modern classification technique. Scientists use this analytical technique to compare the morphological features of species, such as skeletons. In cladistics, organisms are grouped according to their shared characteristics. These shared characteristics confirm the evolutionary links that bind different species into related groups.

8. Another modern technique used to confirm evolutionary relationships is molecular cladistics. Scientists using this technique compare biological elements of different species at the molecular level. Molecular cladistics includes the study of genes and DNA.

9. Scientists cannot reliably obtain actual DNA from fossils that are more than 50,000 years old.

10. Scientists can use computers to work backward from the known DNA of living animals to the likely DNA sequences of their extinct ancestors.

SECTION FOUR:
EARLY LIFE

7

LIFE'S BEGINNINGS

The laws of science can explain many of the fundamental principles that govern life's existence, such as gravity, thermodynamics, molecular biology, and relativity. Much is known about genes, the microscopic engines of metabolic change in organisms. Principles of geophysics explain how the crust of the Earth moves and transforms the face of the planet over spans of time too long for any human to have experienced. Humans can command the laws of mechanics, physics, and chemistry to build incredible motors, vehicles, and artificial fuel that send people traveling to the farthest reaches of the continents and even into outer space. No one, however, can explain how likely it was that life came to exist in the first place.

The chance that life could have sprung forth on a desolate, combustible Earth some 3.5 billion years ago seems less than probable by any measure. Spring forth it did, however, with robust authority, eventually occupying nearly every available nook and cranny of the planet, no matter how seemingly uninhabitable. This chapter explores the development of the earliest life-forms on Earth—the humble origins from which all life on the planet evolved.

PRIMORDIAL ORIGINS OF LIFE

The emergence of life on Earth was tightly bound to the chemical and physical elements of the planet. At the core of all life is a special cocktail of six indispensable chemical elements: oxygen, carbon, hydrogen, nitrogen, sulfur, and phosphorus. Together, these six ingredients make up 95 percent of the mass of nearly all Earthly organisms. These chemical elements originated in the rocks and minerals of the early Earth and are found in organisms and inor-

ganic matter, although in different proportions. During the geologically restless days of the primitive Earth, natural forces combined
and recombined such inorganic elements many times, forming such
materials as minerals and ores and, ultimately, a special concoction
called life.

Making these essential elements available to organisms is largely
the role of water, an unsung hero in the development and persistence of life. Water is not a single element, but a liquid compound
consisting in its purest state of two parts hydrogen to one part oxygen. Water makes up 50 percent to 95 percent of any organism. The
link between water and life is vital. In its natural state, water is commonly found all over the Earth. Furthermore, with the exception
of some archaebacteria, life can survive only within temperature
ranges sustainable by water.

In addition to carrying hydrogen and oxygen, water may transport other elements drawn from the Earth and its atmosphere. It is
significant that the chemicals essential to life are also constituents
of seawater. Water in the form of rain, streams, lakes, and oceans
touches land, causes erosion, permeates rocks and minerals, and
carries with it elements that are essential for life to all environments.
Not surprisingly, the earliest life-forms on Earth arose in the nurturing mineral bath of the oceans.

THE FIRST ORGANISMS

Darwin did not know how the first organisms came into being, but
he understood how natural selection led to the great diversity of
life seen on Earth. In his work *On the Origin of Species by Means of
Natural Selection*, Darwin trusted the logic of his theory of evolution and stated that "all the organic beings which have ever lived
on this Earth may be descended from some one primordial form."
This "primordial form" from which all other life evolved was most
certainly some form of single-celled organism. From those humble
beginnings arose more and more complex plants and animals. The
fossil record bears this out; there are indeed fossils of single-celled
organisms that are simpler than the slightly more complex sponges

and red algae that came later. The sponges, in turn, preceded the more complex **trilobites** and other shelled creatures, which were followed by early sea creatures, fishes, and other vertebrates leading to the wide diversity of life known today.

Fossils can show what early life may have looked like, but fossils do not answer the question of how life first came into being. To find that answer, scientists have conducted experiments to see whether the simplest building blocks of life can be created in the laboratory. One groundbreaking study was conducted in 1953 by American chemist Stanley Miller (1930–2007). Intrigued by Darwin's concept of a "primordial" base from which life arose, Miller simulated the atmosphere of the early Earth in his laboratory equipment. In a flask, Miller combined the chemicals that he thought best represented the state of Earth's atmosphere at the time when life began: water vapor along with methane and ammonia gases. Miller subjected this miniature atmosphere to a constant bombardment of electrical sparks, which he likened to the natural force of lightning. The electrical charges made the gases interact, and the byproducts of these changes were deposited in another flask containing water: Miller's early "ocean." Remarkably, after a few days, a wide variety of organic molecules were indeed created. These included amino acids, the building blocks of proteins and all life. Similar experiments have been done using energy sources other than electrical sparks, such as radiation and ultraviolet light. In these cases, even more complex molecules have been created, including adenine, which is the base of nucleic acid, a component of DNA.

Miller's groundbreaking work demonstrated that the building blocks of life could be created in the lab. Miller, however, did not attempt to explain the actual mechanism responsible for catalyzing these building blocks into single-celled organisms. The solution of that mystery has been the work of two other scientists. Beginning in 1955, American biologist Sidney Fox (1912–1998) extended Miller's work in synthesizing amino acids and demonstrated that when placed in water, proteins could spontaneously self-organize into structures he called "microspheres." His microspheres closely resemble single-celled organisms, including those found in the fossil record.

The complementary work of American Stuart Kauffman (b. 1939) offered a theoretical explanation behind the mingling of inorganic forces seen in the experiments of Miller and Fox. Miller assumed that a basic requirement for the origin of life was that it could arise from inorganic, nonreplicating materials. In other words, life did not originate from a single molecule that already possessed a self-replicating element, such as DNA, but from a set of molecules that, when combined, catalyzed the creation of a new set of molecules that could duplicate themselves. In 1993, Kauffman pioneered a theory suggesting that there was more at work than chance in the rise of such self-replicating molecules. He developed a mathematical basis for predicting the seemingly spontaneous occurrence of order, or **self-organization**, in many kinds of structured "systems," including physics, biology, and economics. Kauffman has shown that such spontaneous order is a "penchant that complex systems have for exhibiting convergent rather than divergent flow," resulting in stability. He believes that the origin of life is just one example of spontaneous order and that the phenomenon of self-organization is as important an element of evolution as natural selection. His work has broadened evolutionary study to consider what happens when natural selection—governed by chance—"acts on systems that already have robust self-organizing properties." Kauffman's work represents a unique new line of thinking in biology.

Research continues on the physical processes that contributed to creating the first biological molecules. In 2004, a team of scientists from the Scripps Research Institute suggested that volcanoes on the ancient Earth may have been the source of raw materials for the building blocks of life. Working in the laboratory, the team successfully used carbonyl sulfide gas—the kind belched out of volcanoes—to string together amino acids, the building blocks of proteins. The scientists were able to make this happen using several kinds of chemical processes, such as combining the gas with oxygen and even with inorganic metals. If this was one of the ways that early biological molecules were created, then lakes near volcanoes or undersea volcanic vents may have been the cradles of early life. These experiments further demonstrated that the components needed to form life could have been created on the early Earth by natural forces.

The processes described by Miller, Fox, Kauffman, and the Scripps researchers provide extraordinary experimental results and models for explaining how life first arose. Fueled by raw materials from volcanoes, the atmosphere, and ocean water, sparked by lightning, heat and perhaps radiation from the Sun, the chemicals in the vast primordial pool of the oceans began to change. All life-forms are composed of cells, and the first organisms were most certainly single-celled bacteria.

FROM SINGLE-CELLED TO MULTICELLED ORGANISMS

The fossil record of the Earth from 2.5 billion to 3.5 billion years ago tells a sketchy but dramatic story of a world undergoing a vast transformation. The early Earth was an inhospitable place where the many kinds of life known today could not have survived. Earth was a hot place. The molten, streaming interior of the planet constantly bubbled up to the surface through volcanic rifts. The atmosphere was made up of carbon dioxide and nitrogen gas and did not contain free oxygen—the most abundant element found in all life-forms. Disruptions in the crust of the planet prevented large landmasses from forming. Planet Earth was largely a vast, roiling, chemical soup.

Despite the seemingly lethal conditions, some forms of single-celled organisms found a niche for themselves in the early oceans. They were cyanobacteria, a form of blue-green algae, and they adapted to survival in a world without oxygen. Fossils of these cyanobacteria consist of rocky mounds called *stromatolites* that exist in areas that were once shallow coastal waters. They are widely distributed around the world in **Precambrian** sedimentary rocks rich in limestone and iron. The bacteria lived in vast colonies, forming a mat that covered the seafloor. The biochemical process of these cells was photosynthesis. Photosynthesizing cells use energy from the Sun, carbon dioxide, and water to produce their own food. As in today's photosynthesizing organisms, the waste product of their biochemical activity was free oxygen released into the atmosphere.

Stromatolite mounds began as a single layer of blue-green algae. As this layer became covered with sediment from wave action in the sea, the algae moved upward toward the Sun, forming another matted layer on top of the previous one. This process went on for years and often resulted in a rocky formation consisting of many layers. Some of these fossil mounds were several yards high. The same process that created them can be seen in action today in living single-celled algae colonies. The earliest stromatolites date from about 3.5 billion years ago and are found in rocks of the Warrawoona Group in Western Australia. When slices of stromatolites are examined under a microscope, they reveal necklacelike beaded structures that were once the home of cyanobacteria. The presence of stromatolites

In some rare instances, stromatolites, layered mounds created by the growth of single-celled photosynthesizing cyanobacteria, are still forming in waters that have a high salt content, such as Shark Bay, Australia.

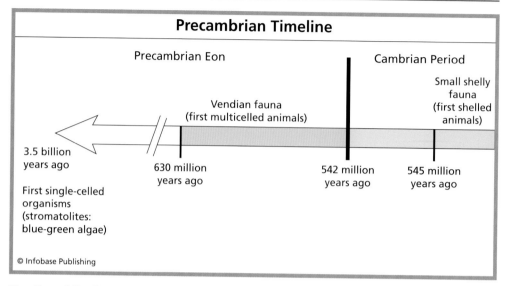

Precambrian Timeline

Precambrian Eon

Cambrian Period

Vendian fauna
(first multicelled animals)

Small shelly
fauna
(first shelled
animals)

3.5 billion
years ago

630 million
years ago

542 million
years ago

545 million
years ago

First single-celled
organisms
(stromatolites:
blue-green algae)

© Infobase Publishing

Timeline of the Precambrian Period

demonstrates that simple forms of life were widespread during the Precambrian Period.

These ancient bacteria were in many ways responsible for the evolution of all life that followed. Without these ocean-dwelling blankets of microbes, the atmosphere may never have become hospitable for the kinds of life that later evolved. Through photosynthesis, bacteria changed the atmosphere of the Earth by filling it with oxygen, the byproduct of their single-cell biochemistry. Around 2 billion years ago, the violent Earth had calmed down, landmasses were stabilizing, and oxygen in the air made for blue skies for the first time. Along the way, a new kind of cell evolved that could use free oxygen for respiration. These cells were the basis of the eukaryotes, the first multicelled organisms, or **metazoans**, that arose in the oceans and set the stage for the wild and extravagant evolution of plant and animal life that followed.

VENDIAN LIFE

Early animals first appear in the fossil record in deposits dating from between 542 million to 630 million years ago. The most

Vendian Body Plans

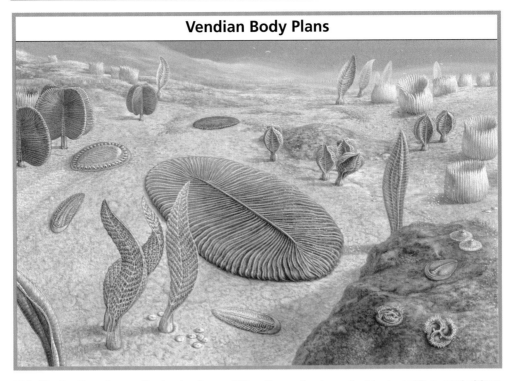

This illustration shows the body plans of Vendian animals: cylindrical, matlike, and either round or rectangular.

distinctive of these fossil specimens consist of external body molds in fine-grained sandstone. They are collectively known as the **Vendian fauna** after a rock formation of the same name in Russia. Excellent remains of **Vendian** creatures have been found in the Ediacara Hills of South Australia, arctic Siberia, the White Sea of northern Russia, Newfoundland, and Namibia. Several modern phyla of animals have roots in the Precambrian Vendian fauna, including sponges, mollusks, jellyfish, and sea stars. These earliest animals, however, do not look much like their modern forms.

The body plans of the Vendian animals were simple and mostly consisted of cylindrical forms or matlike bodies that were either round or rectangular. Vendian creatures had no legs, fins, or other obvious means of moving themselves around.

Some of the best specimens of Vendian fauna are found in the Ediacara Hills of South Australia and date from the end of Precambrian time. Discovered in 1946 by Reginald Sprigg (1919–1994), an Australian mining geologist, the disc-shaped impressions in the rocks were thought by some to have been left by an extinct form of jellyfish. Other scientists thought that the impressions were not fossils at all, but inorganic markings. In 1957, another set of fossils dating from this time were discovered in Leicestershire, England. They resembled modern sea pens, a colonial form of coral with an internal skeletal structure and a long, branchlike shape. Despite the intriguing nature of these separate discoveries in Australia and England, the specimens raised more questions than they answered about this previously unknown period in the development of animals. It took the work of the Czech paleontologist Martin Glaessner (1906–1989) to establish links between these fauna and to have them recognized as the oldest known forms of multicellular life. Glaessner worked in Australia to uncover more fossils in Ediacara. By the 1960s, Glaessner and his associate Mary Wade (1928–2005) were able to show that fossils of Vendian fauna from Australia were related to examples found in England and South Africa. Paleontologists now know that Vendian fossils represent a group of widely diverse species, the first successful spread of multicellular eukaryotes for which there is abundant evidence.

One problem with Vendian fossils is that they often consist of nothing more than a few symmetrical impressions or blobs left in sedimentary rock. Having many examples of these fossils does not necessarily make then any easier to understand. While paleontologists agree that these impressions represent signs of extinct life, the exact nature of the organisms is debatable. What is clear is that Vendian animals were soft-bodied, often were flat and segmented, or had fernlike fronds for a body. Many Vendian organisms did not appear to have any internal organs. Some forms resemble algae, lichen, corals, and simple plants. Others are reminiscent of soft-bodied worms, jellyfish, or arthropods without shells. Some Vendian creatures had a holdfast, a knoblike part of the body that presumably held them in place on the bottom of the ocean. Many Vendian creatures were probably the end run of a line of organisms that no longer exists, a form of life that may never be defined adequately.

About 100 species of Vendian organisms are known. Most of these fossils have been found at the classic sites mentioned earlier: southern Australia, Namibia in South Africa, southern Newfoundland, and the White Sea coast of northern Russia. The distribution of Vendian fossils reaches wider, however—to every continent but Antarctica—and includes notable finds in Brazil, Mexico, England, Ireland, Scandinavia, Ukraine, and the Ural Mountains. Most Vendian creatures were stationary beings, anchored to the seafloor and extracting nutrition from the surrounding water. One group had a unique quilted structure. Their bodies appear to have been composed of radiating strips that look as though they were stitched together, like a patterned quilt. The quilted creatures may have been expandable, like an inflatable mattress. One such example, *Tribrachidium*, is shaped like a pillow with three spiral lobes. Found in Australia, its three-part symmetry is unlike that of modern creatures. Some scientists interpret *Tribrachidium* as a coral; others think that it might have been an anemone or sea star. It is not known whether it swam freely or crawled along the bottom of the sea.

Dickinsonia is another familiar fossil found in the Ediacara formation and in northern Russia. Also a quilted animal, it measured about four inches (10 cm) across and was shaped a little like a flattened piece of fruit. *Dickinsonia* had a dividing line down its axis with quilted strips radiating outward from the axis to its outer edges. It probably coasted along the bottom and may have been a distant relative of the worm.

So-called "quilted" life forms were not alone in the Vendian seas. Many other surprisingly diverse creatures thrived along with them. *Charnia* is the largest of the Vendian fossils discovered so far. This flat creature with a leafy body sometimes reached over three feet (0.9 m) in length. Its branchlike appendage was fastened to the seafloor by a disk-shaped node. *Charnia* is found in central England, Newfoundland, northern Siberia, and Russia and is usually considered to be an ancient relative of the sea pen.

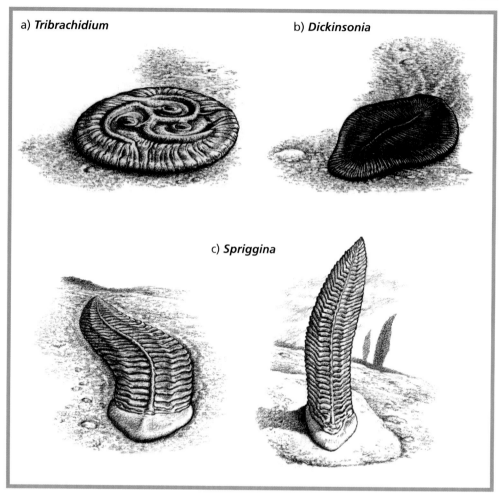

a) *Tribrachidium*

b) *Dickinsonia*

c) *Spriggina*

These illustrations show some of the major examples of Vendian fauna: **a)** *Tribrachidium*, **b)** *Dickinsonia*, **c)** *Spriggina*.

Spriggina is a soft-bodied organism found only in the Vendian fauna. Discovered in the Ediacara Hills of Australia, it appears to have a boomerang-shaped head attached to a series of body segments. Originally thought to be a segmented worm, current thinking suggests that it was an ancestor of the arthropods, perhaps even an early evolutionary experiment in a body type later perfected by trilobites. Unlike many of its Vendian neighbors, *Spriggina* was tiny, measuring only about one inch (3 cm) long. There is also disagreement about the creature's lifestyle. Did it lie flat on the seafloor and crawl, or did it hold itself to the bottom by its boomerang end and wave upright like a plant?

The metabolism of the Vendian fauna is as mysterious as their anatomy. The presence of holdfasts on some of their bodies suggests that they were passive feeders. Like plants, they anchored themselves in one spot. These stationary animals fed on nutrient particles that floated by them in the water. One can picture a seafloor populated with *Spriggina* waving gently in the current. Some Vendian creatures, such as *Dickinsonia*, may have lived within vast colonies of blue-green algae, ingesting the rich quantities of oxygen being given off by these communities of single-celled organisms. Other Vendian organisms, especially those living in the deepest, darkest parts of the sea, where oxygen-rich waters never reached, may have simply absorbed nutrients through their body wall.

VENDIAN EXTINCTION: SETTING THE STAGE FOR AN EXPLOSION OF LIFE

From about 1.6 billion to 2 billion years ago, the top of the planet was shrouded in ice. For millions of years, ice caps stretched down from the North Pole, significantly altering the habitat of Earth's first life forms. This massive polar ice cap was caused by two gradual changes to the Earth. First, the planet was cooling naturally after its hot and restless formative years. Second, the air was becoming rich with free oxygen, the byproduct of the metabolism of worldwide colonies of blue-green algae. Free oxygen created a more uniform atmosphere that reflected a significant amount of incoming heat from the Sun. Had this not happened, the surface of the Earth would have continued to be much warmer. The result of the creation of this more uniform atmosphere was a cooling of the planet that allowed water vapor to freeze and a large polar cap to form.

As these polar ice caps began to melt, they caused widespread changes to the chemistry of the oceans. Sediments rich with nitrogen, sulfides, phosphates, and calcium were released into the seas. Oxygen levels in the air and water were rich and stabilized, encouraging the evolution of multicelled organisms like never before. The presence of calcium as an abundant mineral in the oceans made it possible for shells and eventually bones to develop. Vendian creatures that had long-thrived in an oxygen-deprived ocean disappeared from the fossil record.

Fossils from just before the Cambrian Period provide hints of other creatures that shadowed the quilted and stationary Vendian organisms. The presence of these other creatures is given away by only the slightest of traces. Fossilized burrows and trails in the sea-floor tell of another kind of life-form that was present in the changing oceans. Unlike the familiar Vendian fauna, these soft-bodied creatures could move about. The presence of burrows also suggests that some organisms were escaping from others, making this one of the first signals in the fossil record that some creatures had begun to feed on others. While the origin of many of these trace fossils from the Precambrian is a matter of debate, if they were made by life-forms, they were probably made by early worms and mollusks. Flatworms were probably the first kind of predatory creature. If they were anything like the flatworms that still live today, they were mobile and deadly killers. Soft-bodied, immobile Vendian creatures would have been the perfect prey for flatworms. Sliding along the seafloor, a flatworm would wrap itself around a defenseless quilted animal and slowly suck out the quilted creature's body juices through a tube in the flatworm's mouth.

By about 542 million years ago, the stage of the planet was set for one of the most remarkable acts in the drama of life on Earth. The next chapter explores the wondrous new cast of organisms that sprang up during the Cambrian Period. It was a time of tremendous diversity and experimentation in the melodrama of evolution. The symbiotic relationship between predator and prey would be firmly established, as would the anatomical foundation for the development of the vertebrates.

SUMMARY

This chapter explored the development of the earliest life-forms on Earth—the organisms from which all life on the planet evolved.

1. The earliest form of life from which all other life evolved was single-celled organisms.

2. In 1953, American chemist Stanley Miller successfully demonstrated in a laboratory that the elements found in the atmosphere and oceans of the early Earth could have led to the creation of amino acids, the building blocks of proteins and all life.

3. Beginning in 1955, American biochemist Sidney Fox demonstrated that these proteins could spontaneously self-organize into structures he called "microspheres" when placed in water. His microspheres closely resemble single-celled organisms, including those found in the fossil record.

4. In 1993, American biologist Stuart Kauffman developed a mathematical basis for predicting the seemingly spontaneous occurrence of order, or self-organization, in many kinds of structured "systems." He suggested that the origin of life is just one example of spontaneous order and that the phenomenon of self-organization is as important an element of evolution as natural selection.

5. The earliest form of life known from the fossil record are stromatolites, photosynthesizing bacterial colonies that lived in shallow ocean waters. They date from 3.5 billion years ago.

6. The Vendian fauna represent the most distinctive fossil record of the first known animals. They date from about 542 billion to 630 million years ago.

7. The melting of ice caps near the end of the Precambrian Period caused widespread changes to the chemistry of the oceans. This led to an explosion of new life-forms in the Cambrian Period.

8. The first evidence of the evolution of predatory animals is found in the Vendian fauna.

An Explosion of Life

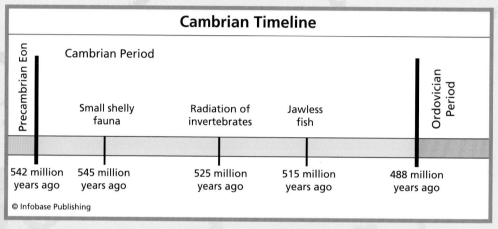

Cambrian Timeline

Precambrian Eon	Cambrian Period			**Ordovician Period**
	Small shelly fauna	Radiation of invertebrates	Jawless fish	

| 542 million years ago | 545 million years ago | 525 million years ago | 515 million years ago | 488 million years ago |

© Infobase Publishing

Timeline of life in the Cambrian Period

Precambrian rocks contain fossils of the oldest known organisms. The Vendian fauna and other lesser understood life-forms from that time show that Earth's oceans were becoming home to many kinds of single-celled and multicelled organisms. The most striking and best understood of the Vendian fauna, however, became extinct. As the curtain came down on their turn on Earth's stage, life took several new directions, ultimately leading to the kinds of creatures known in today's world.

The Cambrian Period is remarkable for many reasons. It marked the first appearance in the fossil record of multicelled organisms with hard parts such as shells and exoskeletons. The Cambrian was the beginning of an escalating arms race between predator and prey. Perhaps most amazingly, however, the Cambrian period witnessed an explosion of diverse life-forms that laid the foundation for all major animal phyla that exist today. This chapter explores those organisms, their relationship to today's life, and ways in which the discovery of the Cambrian fauna has influenced thinking about evolution.

CAMBRIAN CONTINENTS AND CLIMATES

The warming of the climate at the end of the Precambrian Period melted glaciers and flooded the world with mineral-rich waters. Much of the land that had been dry during the Precambrian Period was now flooded by warm shallow seas. The world was swimming into a new phase in the evolution of life.

By the end of the Cambrian Period, 488 million years ago, the super continent Gondwana had formed. Gondwana was located south of the equator and would later break apart to become the continents of South America, Africa, and Antarctica. Other, smaller landmasses included Laurentia, Baltica, and Siberia; those parts of the crust that would one day become North America.

The worldwide climate of the Cambrian was mild and moderately warm, with abundant rainfall. There was little ice formation. The oceans were vast and teeming with minerals, oxygen, and nutrients to feed the development of new species.

SMALL SHELLY ANIMALS OF THE EARLY CAMBRIAN

The Cambrian Period began quietly with the emergence of what have been called the **small shelly faunas,** tiny but abundant creatures represented by the hard parts they left behind. The best specimens of the small shellies have been found in South Australia and Yunnan Province, China. Small cones, jesterlike hats, cups, and snail-like shells are the only clues to whatever once lived during that time. The small shellies measured only 0.2 inches (5 mm) in length and were most likely early mollusks with creeping feet, like those of snails, for moving about the ocean floor. The fact that they had shells suggests that they had found a way to defend against predatory flatworms.

Small Shelly Fauna

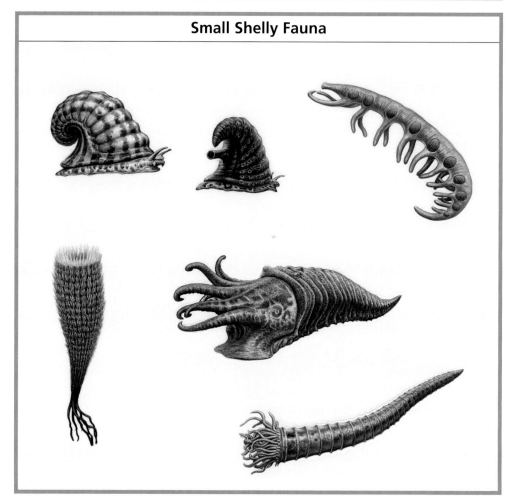

Small shelly fauna were usually less than one inch long. Their hard parts probably protected them from predators.

A second group of organisms that lived at the same time were the archaeocyathids. Instead of cuplike shells, their hard parts consisted of porous, sievelike outer shells. The most common of these archaeocyathans were upright forms that gathered to create reef-like barriers in the shallow ocean. Their hard parts consisted of a cup within a cup—both with tiny holes for filtering water and nutrients. They probably held themselves fast to the seafloor and may have had soft tissue inside the cups much like that of a sponge. Another

form of archaeocyathid resembled a tubular worm with pairs of fin-
gerlike legs. It, too, had a porous outer covering of sieve plates.

Additional evidence for early Cambrian life comes in the form of
tiny nodes, scales, and hornlike structures. It is sometimes impossible to connect these fragmentary fossils with specific creatures,
but an amazing discovery in Early Cambrian rocks in Greenland
shed light on one of these organisms. *Halkieria*, discovered in 1990,
looked like a hot dog with an outer covering of overlapping scales
and a cup-shaped shell capping each end of its body. *Halkieria* probably crawled through the ocean-bottom sediment by contracting its
muscles.

AN EXPLOSION OF LIFE

Paleontologists refer to the Middle Cambrian Period as the "Cambrian explosion" of life. The first remarkable fossils from this time
period came from a single quarry in the Canadian Rocky Mountains of British Columbia. Found in Yoho National Park, the fossil
site is known as the Burgess Shale. Shale is sedimentary rock formed
by layers of clay or mud. The organisms found in the Burgess Shale
lived in relatively shallow water and were probably trapped in small
underwater mudflows. This occurred at a time when the sea in
which they lived was near the equator, on the outer edge of what
would become North America. Most of the Burgess Shale fossils
have been collected from a single, small quarry outcrop no taller
than a person and extending only about 200 feet (60 m) in length.
That is no longer than a small pond.

Thousands of exquisitely detailed remains have been found in
the Burgess Shale since its discovery by Charles Walcott (1850–1927)
in 1909. It was the discovery of a lifetime for Walcott, who was 59
at the time. In the 18 years that followed, he described 119 genera
and about 150 species from this quarry. Not all of Walcott's original species are currently recognized. A good number have since
been proved to be members of already named species. This is not
to discredit Walcott, for the world of animals he was examining
was totally unknown at the time. The alien appearance and often

fragmentary specimens of many of these organisms made them difficult to identify. Sometimes a part of one animal might be mistaken for another. The process of detecting and correcting errors is a familiar part of science. Walcott's pioneering efforts laid the groundwork for many paleontologists who followed him into an exploration of the Cambrian fauna. New members of the Burgess Shale fauna continue to be discovered to this day.

Other Important Cambrian Fossil Sites

About 75 years after the discovery of the Burgess Shale, two other significant deposits of Cambrian fossils were discovered, one in China and the other in Greenland.

In 1984, paleontologist Hou Xian-Guang was prospecting for fossils near the town of Chengjiang in the Yunnan Province of southern China. The sedimentary rock in this area goes back to the Early Cambrian. Hou was casually breaking open mudstone rocks to see whether any contained fossils. One can do this for many days without ever finding anything. But one rock revealed a small but magnificent fossil about the length of a large paper clip. The rocks were about 20 million years younger than those of the Burgess Shale. Startled by his good fortune, Hou immediately realized the possible significance of this discovery. In his excitement, Hou took the specimen home and put it under his bed for safekeeping until morning. The very presence of the fossil haunted Hou all night. "Because I was so excited, I couldn't sleep very well. I got up often and pulled out the fossils just to look at them." What lay under his bed were the remains of a life-form that was half a billion years old. His sleepless night paid off big-time. Since that time, thousands of exquisite specimens of shelled and soft-bodied marine fossils have been discovered at the Chengjiang site.

Unbelievably, only one day after Hou's discovery, another important fossil site was found near a fjord in the far north of Greenland. Now dubbed Sirius Passet, this site also dated from the Early Cambrian but was not quite as old as the Chengjiang locality.

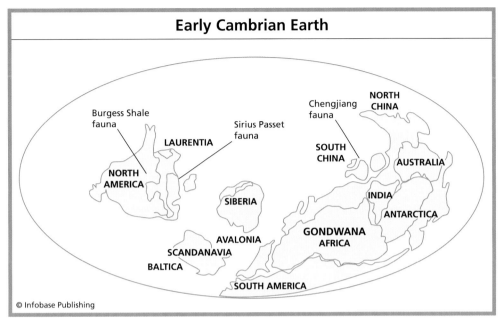

Early Cambrian Earth

Burgess Shale fauna

LAURENTIA

Sirius Passet fauna

NORTH AMERICA

SIBERIA

AVALONIA

SCANDANAVIA

BALTICA

SOUTH AMERICA

Chengjiang fauna

NORTH CHINA

SOUTH CHINA

AUSTRALIA

INDIA

ANTARCTICA

GONDWANA AFRICA

© Infobase Publishing

This map shows the major sites of Cambrian fossils, including the Burgess Shale (Canada), Sirius Passet (Greenland), and Chengjiang (China).

Sirius Passet, too, has yielded a wealth of magnificent specimens, although they are not quite as well preserved as the Burgess Shale and Chengjiang fossils.

The fossil sites in China and Greenland create a more complete picture of the Cambrian Period. Geographically, the submerged areas of the Earth that would become western Canada, northern Greenland, and southern China were widely separated. Greenland was, in fact, closer to the equator.

The creatures of these three widely spaced localities are also similar. The animals of Chengjiang are so like those of the Burgess Shale that each site seems like a direct extension of the other. Many of the fossils found at Chengjiang represent additional and earlier species of animals found in the Burgess Shale. One of the first Chinese specimens analyzed was an **onychophoran** that helped show that Canada's *Hallucigenia* had unwittingly been turned on its back. Chengjiang has also revealed several more species of the predator

Anomalocaris as well as a number of early **chordates** that predate *Pikaia* from Canada. The Sirius Passet fossils are not quite as plentiful, and there are few trilobites there, but, like the Canadian and Chinese localities, Sirius Passet has more specimens of early arthropods than anything else. Together, all three localities provide clues to an explosive burst of evolution during a time that was only the blink of an eye by geologic standards.

SIGNIFICANT FOSSIL DEPOSITS OF THE CAMBRIAN PERIOD

Locality	Age	Fauna
Chengjiang, in Yunnan Province, China. Discovered in 1984 by Hou Xian-Guang.	Early Cambrian (525 mya)	About 100 species, including sponges, cnidarians, ctenophores, nematomorph and priapulid worms, hyolithids, lobopodians, many arthropod groups, trilobites, anomalocarids, brachiopods, several chordates, and additional forms that are less understood
Sirius Passet, northern coast of Greenland. Discovered in 1984 by A.K. Higgins.	Early Cambrian (505 mya to 518 mya)	More than 20 species, including many arthropod groups, sponges, brachiopods, annelids, trilobites, and priapulids
Burgess Shale, British Columbia, Canada. Discovered by Charles Walcott in 1909.	Middle Cambrian (505 mya)	About 140 species, including green and red algae, sponges, brachiopods, priapulids, annelids, many arthropod groups, echinoderms, an early chordate, and other puzzlers

SIGNIFICANCE OF THE CAMBRIAN PHYLA

Together, the fossils from the Burgess Shale, Chengjiang, and Sirius Passet provide remarkable evidence for the "explosive" nature of Cambrian evolution. These life-forms probably had roots as early as the Precambrian, but what makes their evolution "explosive" is the variety and number of species that evolved during the short geologic span—about 15 million years—for which there is fossil evidence.

There are currently about 23 recognized phyla of living animals. Remembering the hierarchy of classification defined by Carolus Linnaeus, phyla are the largest generally accepted groupings, after kingdoms, of organisms that share similar anatomical features. Phyla are found in the kingdoms of plants and animals. Members of a phylum are like one another in the broadest sense. Some familiar animal phyla are mollusks (such as clams), arthropods (such as insects), and the chordates (vertebrates and their relatives). In the tree of life, phyla are the biggest branches leading from the trunk. When a new dinosaur is discovered, it does not represent a new phylum; it is a member of the phylum Chordata, which is further broken down at the class level into fishes, amphibians, reptiles, mammals, and birds. A particular kind of dinosaur, or any other individual member of a given animal group, is further down the list of categories of classification, at the species level. While discovering a new species of dinosaur is fantastic, it is not as unusual as discovering a new phylum of animals. Discovering a new phylum is exceedingly rare because one must find a kind of animal that is entirely different from all others in nearly all respects—a kind of animal that is unrelated to every other kind of animal known at present. When a claim is made about the discovery of a new phylum, it often happens on the discovery of an unusual, previously unknown species.

Knowing about phyla helps put the remarkable animals of the Cambrian Period in perspective. The Cambrian fossils found in three relatively small fossil quarries in Canada, China, and Greenland represented the ancestors of nearly all 23 modern animal phyla. Equally significant, the Burgess Shale fauna include 20 additional kinds of extinct creatures that are so wildly different from today's organisms that they cannot be placed in any known modern phyla of animals.

The Burgess Shale also teaches an important lesson about evolution. Evolution does not always lead to more and better versions of what came before. The explosion of life in the Middle Cambrian went in many directions at once. Based on what is seen in the

Burgess Shale, there were nearly twice as many kinds or phyla of animals at the beginning of animal evolution than there are now. Many, however, such as the trilobites and halkieriids, became extinct—unable to adapt well enough to changes in their world.

Cambrian fossil sites represent only a small portion of an ancient worldwide ecosystem. The fact that so many strange and different animals were found in only three small fossil mud holes suggests that many other kinds of creatures were alive and well during the same time elsewhere on Earth. The areas represented by the Burgess Shale, Chengjiang, and Sirius Passet were mere drops in the vast bucket of the fully habitable Cambrian oceans. There were most certainly other kinds of habitats, with deeper waters, different temperatures, other creatures, and promising opportunities for evolving life. It is impossible to know how many other kinds of animals actually existed back then, which makes fossils of the Cambrian Period paleontology's biggest tease.

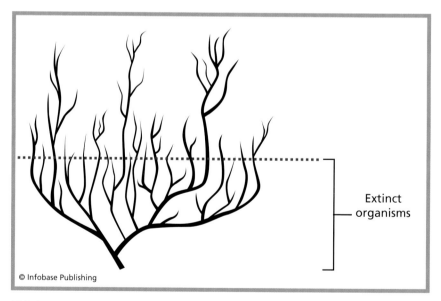

Extinct organisms

© Infobase Publishing

This hypothetical phylogenetic tree suggests the diversity of life that may have existed during the Cambrian Period, represented by the portion of the tree below the dashed line. Many of these family lines of organisms have since become extinct, resulting in a tree of life that is considerably sparser than in the past.

THE BURGESS SHALE AND THE SPEED OF MIDDLE CAMBRIAN EVOLUTION

Although one can think of evolution as taking an enormous amount of time, this is not always the case when one calculates according to geologic standards. The animals of the Burgess Shale evolved during a geologically short span of time. It is remarkable to think that nearly all of today's animal phyla originated during a 15 million-year period from 525 to 540 million years ago. In only a few million years, the rate of evolution and the variety of life expanded immensely. There are several reasons for such rapid evolution.

The number of evolutionary changes that take place in a species are affected, first, by the life span of the species. Evolution can continue only as genes are passed from one generation to the next. When measured on the scale of human time, animals with shorter life spans can evolve more quickly than those with longer life spans. This may not guarantee more success: Evolution does not always lead to better survival. But a shorter life span makes it possible for changes to occur in a species more quickly than it occurs in other animals with longer life spans.

Species also appear capable of evolving rapidly and spectacularly when new habitats appear. What made rapid evolution possible in the Cambrian was the warming of the Earth, the rising of sea levels, and the creation of new habitats offering unlimited opportunities. The advent of multicelled animals also accelerated as the lines between predator and prey were drawn for the first time in life's early history. The arms race that followed favored traits that either protected species from their enemies or enabled those enemies to hunt their prey more effectively. The development for the first time of hard outer shells and of stronger bodies capable of moving about were probably the first stages in this arms race.

Rapid evolution has happened more than once in Earth's past. One well-studied example is that of cichlid fishes in Lake Malawi, a freshwater lake in East Africa. During the past 700,000 years, more

(continues on page 174)

THINK ABOUT IT

Today's Phyla with Roots in the Cambrian

Almost all of today's major animal groups have roots in the Cambrian. The rich fossil evidence provided by the Burgess Shale can tell us much about evolution since that time. As different as many of the Cambrian creatures seem to be, they provide vital clues to early forms of most phyla of animals that are alive today. This is because evolution reveals that today's animals have some ancestral forms in common. As these ancestral animals evolved over time into more and different species, they became less and less alike. Many basic anatomical features that distinguished these ancestral animals from one another during the Cambrian Period are still somewhat intact, however. For example, the ocean-dwelling Cambrian velvet worms *Hallucigenia* and *Aysheaia* are similar in many of their details to velvet worms that live today. The primary difference is that today's varieties are strictly terrestrial: They are land animals. Cambrian arthropods, although superficially quite different in appearance from today's arthropods, established many of the anatomical rules that make up their taxa, such as segmented bodies and jointed exoskeletons. These clues and links between the fossil record and today's animals allow paleontologists to establish evolutionary relationships between them.

To understand the kinds of animals found in the Burgess Shale fossils, it helps to understand the phyla of invertebrates that are still around today. What is known about living invertebrates provides an enormous set of clues to the lives and habits of their very distant and extinct ancestors.

The following is a breakdown of living invertebrate phyla that have roots in the Cambrian Period.

Arthropods. Members of this phylum have a segmented body, body regions dedicated to specific functions (the head for feeding, the abdomen for housing major organs, and the thorax for locomotion), a jointed exoskeleton, and a nervous system on the underside of the body. Arthropods account for at least 75 percent of all animal species alive today. Their members include predators, **deposit feeders** (organisms that get their food from the seafloor), and **scavengers** (organisms that feed on the dead remains of other organisms). Trilobites, now extinct, were a widespread member of this phyla during the Cambrian Period. Today's arthropods include crabs, lobsters, brine shrimp, barnacles, insects, spiders, scorpions, and centipedes.

Annelids. Members of this phylum have fluid-filled, segmented bodies, are worm-shaped, have a nervous system on the underside of the body, and possess at least one pair of hairlike bristles. Many marine **annelids** have eyes and tentacles and burrow into the sediment. Feeding habits of worms vary widely and include **predation** (feeding on other live animals), scavenging, **suspension feeding** (filtering out food particles floating around them), and deposit feeding (eating deposits of organic matter, usually in mud). Today's annelids include worms that live on the land and in the sea, and leeches.

Onychophora. These predatory animals—velvet worms—feed on small arthropods. They capture their prey by discharging a slimy glue from their mouth appendages. This glue holds the victim fast while the velvet worm feeds on it. A suggestion has recently been made to reclassify the Onychophora to include extinct marine forms. A new phylum, the **Lobopodia**, would include two classes, the extinct Xenusia for marine forms, and the Onychophora, now a phylum, for terrestrial forms.

Chordata. Members of this phylum possess a **notochord,** which is a stiff rod running along the back. Chordates also have a nerve cord running on top of the notochord, gill slits for breathing, and a tail. All living chordates are marine animals. Most are filter feeders, but a few are predators. They include lancelets, salps, ascidians, and larvaceans.

Poriferans. The **poriferans,** or sponges, are one of the simplest yet most successful creatures on Earth, with between 5,000 and 10,000 species known today. Their cells are not organized into tissues or organs, but are composed primarily of chambers for channeling water. Many poriferans have bodies that are shapeless blobs; there is no such thing as up, down, or sideways to these types. Other kinds of sponges have

(continues)

(continued)

The small velvet worm, *Peripatopsis*, is from the Onychophora phylum.

extremely symmetrical structures. All poriferans are stationary suspension feeders.

Cnidarians. This phylum includes marine animals whose bodies consist of a large central chamber that receives and digests food. The **cnidarians** have a single opening that serves as both the mouth and the anus. Cnidarians have two radically different body plans. The medusa form is a large, bulbous, baglike structure that swims. The polyp form has a tubular body and is usually fixed in a stationary position. All members of this phylum have a distinctive radial symmetry, with parts arranged in a regular pattern around a central axis, and have only two layers of living tissue. All cnidarians have tentacles around the mouth and are carnivorous suspension feeders. Members of this phylum include corals, jellyfish, sea anemones, sea fans, sea pens, and the Portuguese man-of-war.

Priapulids. This phylum includes only 15 known species of tiny, carnivorous worms. **Priapulids** live in muddy sediment. Most are only a few millimeters long, but individuals in some species may reach eight inches (20 cm) in length. Priapulids have unsegmented, tubular bodies. They move freely and are often found gathered in their own communities in the mud. Some members of this phylum are predatory; others are deposit feeders. They appear to have been more common in the Middle Cambrian than they are today.

Sipuncula. This phylum includes marine worms that have been found living in both shallow and deep sea habitats. Members of the phylum Sipuncula—called **sipunculans,** or sipuncular worms—have plump, peanut-shaped, unsegmented bodies with a long mouth appendage that can be retracted into the body. The tip of the mouth is lined with tentacles for gathering food. The bodies of sipuncular worms are muscular, with a hard outer covering. Sipunculans are deposit feeders. They can dig burrows.

Invertebrates that have roots in the Cambrian Period include the jellyfish (a), anemone (b), and coral (c).

(continued from page 169)

than 400 species have evolved in this lake from a single species of ancestor. When these fish first appeared in the lake, they adapted rapidly to the new, wide-open environment. Species developed in different directions, with some becoming more stationary bottom feeders while others took to the rocky nooks and crannies in other parts of the lake. Fish species evolved as opportunities in the habitat permitted. The story of the Cambrian explosion may have been similar.

Other factors may have encouraged the Cambrian's rapid evolution of new life-forms. One theory suggests that higher oxygen levels in the air spurred the growth and development of multicellular organisms. Another factor may have been changes in the chemistry and temperature of seawater that favored a wider variety of life-forms than had lived in Vendian times. None of these theories, however, is universally accepted. The Cambrian explosion may always be one of the most puzzling enigmas of prehistoric life.

UNDERSTANDING THE BURGESS SHALE

Illustrations of the Burgess Shale creatures offer views of a life that is alien in many ways to the life of the present time. Many of the Burgess Shale animals do not fit neatly into our images of what animals should be. While one tends to think of prehistoric life forms as having been supersized when compared with their modern counterparts, this was not always the case, as the marvelous Burgess Shale shows.

Gigantic monsters did not rule the Middle Cambrian oceans. It was a time of small life-forms, most of which were only a few inches long. About 14 percent of the animals had shells; the rest were soft-bodied. The largest free-swimming animal was the predator *Anomalocaris*, which was about two feet (60 cm) long. The largest stationary feeder was the plantlike *Thaumaptilon*, a form of sea pen that reached the unimpressive height of eight inches (10 cm). The majority of the other creatures were small, crawling, creeping, and burrowing deposit feeders. *Anomalocaris* was enormous by Middle Cambrian standards, and one can imagine it hovering over the sea-

This illustration reflects the misconception that prehistoric creatures were large and menacing. The largest creatures during the Middle Cambrian were probably about two feet long.

floor like the a blimp, snatching up its daily share of tiny, scampering creatures.

The kinds of fossil creatures found in the Burgess Shale also offer information about the habitat in which they lived. While about 88 percent of the fossils are animals, most of the rest are algae. Knowing that algae need a healthy amount of sunlight for photosynthesis, the entire collection of Burgess organisms must have lived in shallow water, no more than 300 feet (90 m) deep at its deepest. Most of the animals of the Burgess Shale were bottom feeders that probably did not move much. A small percentage of them were free-swimming, including several predatory creatures. Most of the kinds of creatures we see today, on land or in the sea, have their roots in the oceans of the Middle Cambrian Period.

About 140 species of creatures are currently recognized from the wondrous Burgess Shale. Rather than being squashed flat like roadkill, many of the Burgess Shale specimens are three-dimensional. They provide glimpses of the top, bottom, and sides of organisms as well as their general body volume. This rare state of fossilization provides paleontologists with an unprecedented view of ancient life.

The creatures of the Burgess Shale environment can be broadly divided into two ecological niches: those creatures that lived on or near the bottom of the sea and did little or no swimming, and those that freely swam about. Of the 140 Burgess Shale species, about a third are currently believed to be ancestors of the arthropods, the phylum of animals that includes insects, crustaceans, and spiders.

BURGESS SHALE ANIMALS AND THEIR PHYLA

Species	Current Phylum	Extinct Phylum
Anomalocaris	--	Unknown lineage
Aysheaia	Onychophora (velvet worms)	--
Canadia	Annelids	--
Canadaspis	Arthropods (crabs)	--
Hallucigenia	Onychophora (velvet worms)	--
Leanchoilia	Arthropods	--
Marrella	Arthropods	--
Naraoia	--	Arthropods (trilobites)
Olenoides	--	Arthropods (trilobites)
Opabinia	--	Unknown lineage
Perspicaris	Arthropods (crabs)	--
Pikaia	Chordates	--
Sidneyia	Arthropods	--
Thaumaptilon	Cnidarians (sea pens)	--
Wiwaxia	--	Unknown lineage

Lifestyles of the Burgess Organisms

The Burgess organisms were represented by 15 to 20 unique kinds of body plans, some of which have not been seen since. Despite their unique anatomy, most of these creatures fell into one of the three lifestyles that are still seen in ocean creatures today: deposit feeders, suspension feeders, and predators and scavengers.

Deposit Feeders

Mud eating is widely used by animals that live on the seafloor. Mud contains deposits of organic matter—parts of dead or dying animals and plants that have fallen to the bottom. Mud also contains feces—bodily waste—from other animals, a source of possible nutrients because of bits of undigested organic matter that are left behind.

Deposit feeders come in two varieties. The first type are the animals that swallow big gulps of mud, digest whatever they can from it, and then pass the rest out as feces. The second type of deposit feeders are the collectors. Rather than taking in mouthfuls of mud, collectors use appendages such as tentacles or arms to pick up or shovel bits of mud into their mouths.

Eating mud is not a delicate science, so deposit feeders need little precision. Any way they can get the mud into their mouths is usually good enough. Some Cambrian deposit feeders may have burrowed into the mud with their mouths wide open. Others may have had tiny, sticky hairs on their arms to pick-up bits of mud. Some also may have filtered out larger bits of mud with sievelike mouths or screens.

Suspension Feeders

In suspension feeding, organisms remove food particles floating through the water by catching them, trapping them, or filtering them out. Once caught, the food is passed into the feeder's mouth area for consumption. This is a common feeding technique used by many invertebrates, including sponges, jellyfish, brachiopods, and bivalves, such as clams and oysters. Some suspension, or filter, feeders may swim actively so that food particles suspended in the water will pass by their mouth area. Others may remain still, relying on currents to bring the food to them. Some Burgess Shale creatures may have lacked a single mouth, instead absorbing food through many surface locations on their bodies.

Predators and Scavengers

Predation is feeding on other live animals. Predation is the most sophisticated form of feeding because it requires the capture of live prey. **Predators** may be designed to capture one prey at a time—the case with many of the Burgess Shale creatures—or may be designed to consume large numbers of smaller prey by sweeping over an area and scooping them up almost aimlessly.

Not every animal hunts or stalks its prey in the same way. Active stalkers are on the lookout for prey all the time, moving about to find them. Modern examples include certain worms, gastropods, octopuses, squids, and the big cats. Lurking predators sit still and wait for prey to come to them. Praying mantises, crabs, spiders, and many vertebrates use this style of predation. Stationary predators do not move much at all and can seize prey only when it comes in contact with them. Barnacles, anemones, and corals are stationary predators.

Scavengers are animals that feed on the dead remains of other organisms. Some predators may turn to scavenging if the opportunity arises, and some scavengers may turn to predation. Crawfish, for example, are scavengers most of the time. If a lazy fish swims within reach, however, a crawfish may snatch it with its claws.

THE *WHO'S WHO* OF THE BURGESS SHALE

It is difficult to divide the creatures of the Burgess Shale into neat groups because many of the creatures differ so much from one another. One simple way to categorize them is by lifestyle. The following descriptions are therefore divided into three categories based on how these creatures fed: deposit feeders, suspension feeders, and predatory and scavenging feeders.

Deposit Feeders

Marrella was first thought to be an early trilobite, one of the most familiar fauna of the Late Cambrian Period. This early arthropod is

(continues on page 182)

THINK ABOUT IT

The Scientific Naming Game

A rose may be a rose, but a *Rosa gymnocarpa* is a particular kind of rose unlike any other. Rose is the common name for this flower. *Rosa gymnocarpa* is the scientific name for a particular species of rose.

A common name is good for categories of things but does not clearly distinguish between one type of thing and another in the same category. For example, there are mountains all over the planet, but there is only one Mount Everest. Any kind of rose may be called a *rose*, but if a scientist wants to talk about a specific kind of wood rose, he or she uses the scientific name *Rosa gymnocarpa*.

The scientific name of a species contains two words. Both are derived from the Linnaean tradition of classification. The first word is the genus name and is capitalized. The second word is the species name and is not capitalized. Both the genus and species parts of the two-part name are italicized. In the science of taxonomy, every species of living thing has only one, unambiguous scientific name.

Fossil organisms are named using the same international rules that govern the naming of living species. The scientist who first describes a species in a scientific publication is given the honor of naming it. The name is usually in Latin but often may include a "Latinized" version of a word from another language. The reason for using a common language—in this case, Latin—to name species is so that scientists all over the world can use the same names. A Russian botanist, for example, will use the same scientific name for a rose as a botanist from China or any other country.

A scientific name is meaningful. It can tell something about a species. The first thing a scientific name shows is how a given species is related to other species. As in the example of the rose, a genus (*Rosa*) may have more than one species. Every kind of rose has the generic name of *Rosa* followed by a unique species name: *gymnocarpa* for the wood rose, or *californica* for the California rose, for example.

(continues)

(continued)

A scientific name may also reveal something that makes the given species unique. A species might be named after the place where it was found, the rock formation in which it was deposited, or something about its anatomy. In some cases, the name may tell something about the imagined behavior of a fossil organism. Once in a while, a scientist will honor a person by naming a species after him or her. A scientist, however, never names a species after him- or herself. To do so would be considered very bad manners.

This book generally uses only the genus name of a species to refer to a specific kind of extinct organism. Here are some examples, all from the Burgess Shale, of complete species names and their meanings.

SOME ORGANISMS FROM THE BURGESS SHALE

Scientific Name (Genus/species)	Pronunciation	Meaning of Name
Anomalocaris canadensis	ah-NOME-ah-LAH-kariss KAN-ah-DEN-sis	"Unusual Canadian shrimp," from the Greek word *anomalos* ("unusual") and the Greek word *caris* ("shrimp")
Aysheaia pedunculata	*eye-SHAY-ah pee-DUNK-yoo-LAH-ta*	After Ayshea, a mountain peak in British Columbia, Canada, and *peduncle*, a Latin word meaning "small foot"
Canadia spinosa	ka-NAY-dee-ah spine-OZE-ah	"The Spiny Canadian," after Canada and the Latin word *spinosa* ("sharp point"; "spiny")
Hallucigenia sparsa	hahl-loo-sih-GEEN-ee-ah SPARS-ah	"Dreamlike," from the Latin *hallucina* ("hallucination"; "to wander in the mind")
Leanchoilia superlata	LEE-an-COY-lee-ah sue-PURR-lah-tah	After Leanchoil, a railroad station in Canada, and the Latin word *superlata* ("superior")
Marrella splendens	marr-ELL-ah SPLEN-denz	In honor of paleontologist J.E. Marr and from the Latin word *splendens* ("shining"; "brilliant")

Scientific Name (Genus/species)	Pronunciation	Meaning of Name
Naraoia compacta	Nair-OYE-yah com-PACK-tah	After the Narao Lakes in British Columbia and the Latin word *compacta* ("small")
Olenoides serratus	OH-len-OY-deez sair-AH-tuss	After Olenus, the husband of Lethaea, both of whom, in Greek mythology, were turned to stone, and the Latin word *serratus* ("saw-shaped") for the animal's spines
Opabinia regalis	OH-pah-BIN-nee-ah ree-GAL-is	"King Opabin," after Opabin, a mountain pass in British Columbia, and the Latin word *regalis* ("like a king")
Pikaia gracilens	pih-KAY-ah GRASS-ih-lenz	After Mount Pika in British Columbia and the Latin word *gracilens* ("slender"; "thin")
Sidneyia inexpectans	SID-nee-ah in-ex-PECK-tanz	"Sidney's discovery," after paleontologist Charles Walcott's son Sidney, who discovered the specimen, and the Latin *inexpectans* ("unexpected")
Thaumaptilon walcotti	THAW-mah-TILL-on WALL-kot-eye	"Walcott's wonderful sea feather," from the Greek *thauma* ("marvel"); the Greek *ptilon* ("feather" or "leaf"); and Walcott, after Charles Walcott, who discovered the Burgess Shale deposits
Wiwaxia corrugata	why-WAX-ee-ah CORE-yoo-GAH-tah	After Wiwaxy, a small mountain peak in British Columbia, and the Latin word *corrugatus* ("ridged"; "wrinkled")

(continued from page 178)

one of the most common fossil animals found in the Burgess Shale, with more than 15,000 examples currently in hand. This small creature was no more than three-quarters of an inch (2 cm) long. The abundant presence of *Marrella* in the Burgess Shale deposits suggests that it must have been highly successful. The body was composed of jointed segments and many small legs. Equipped with two pairs of long spines, its head reminds one of a trophy set from a longhorn steer. *Marrella* fed on small animals and other organic material as it cruised along the bottom sediment. Its connection to modern phyla of arthropods is unknown, but *Marrella* may be an ancestor to any one of three groups: the crustaceans, the scorpions and spiders, or the trilobites.

Fortunately for science, not all of the strange, otherworldly Burgess Shale creatures are totally disconnected from animals known today. If they were, this explosion of evolution in the Middle Cambrian would be known only as a dead-end. Instead, some of these animals turn out to be remarkable prototypes of animals that are still with us. An excellent example is *Canadaspis*, one of the earliest known relatives of the crustaceans—crabs and lobsters. *Canadaspis* is known from more than 4,000 specimens, making it the second most common animal fossil from the Middle Cambrian, after *Marrella*. *Canadaspis* bears many of the telltale signs of the modern members of the phylum Arthropoda. What reveals *Canadaspis* as a true crustacean is its five-segment head with two eyes, two antennae, and three appendages behind the mouth opening. The jaws or mouth parts of arthropods are actually legs that shovel food into the mouth cavity, and *Canadaspis* was no exception. The head and forward part of its segmented body were covered by an outer shell, or carapace. Its segmented abdomen stuck out the back, looking much like the tail of a lobster. *Canadaspis* had eight pairs of small legs for walking along the seafloor. Each leg had a frilly gill flap to enable *Canadaspis* to breathe. But *Canadaspis* was not lobster size. At about three inches (8 cm) long, it was only about crawfish size.

Canadaspis probably ate large gulps of sea mud and extracted food particles from it.

Yohoia was named after Yoho National Park, Canada, where the Burgess Shale is found. This small, free-swimming creature does not fit neatly into any known group of arthropods. *Yohoia* lacked the many legs and antennae normally found in arthropods and had a unique design all its own. *Yohoia's* segmented body was narrow and covered with a series of overlapping plates like the shell of a shrimp. The first 10 body segments had a small flap underneath, covered with fine, hairlike filaments. These flaps may have done double duty as gills and as tiny appendages for swimming. The last five segments of the body narrowed into a shrimplike tail. The head segment had three pairs of tiny legs that may have helped *Yohoia* get a grip when it was not swimming. *Yohoia* also had two large eyes and a pair of unique jointed limbs in the front. Each of these tiny limbs was capped with four tiny spikes, presumably for spearing prey. *Yohoia* was a rarity in the Burgess Shale fauna: a free-swimming predator.

Burgessia was another mud-eating deposit feeder. Like *Canadaspis*, this animal looks like a prototype of modern arthropods. Like *Yohoia*, however, *Burgessia* is such a hodgepodge of different kinds of arthropod parts that it is impossible to link it with certainty to any known group of living crustaceans, insects, or other arthropods. *Burgessia* had an oval shell that covered its body, a long tail spike, and two long antennae. The underside had 10 pairs of legs. The rear half of the body consisted of seven tapering segments, each equipped with a pair of gill lobes.

Leanchoilia was an arthropod with similarities to spiders, scorpions, and trilobites. The two-inch (5 cm) creature did not have eyes. *Leanchoilia* was oval-shaped, with a large, triangular head, a body with 11 segments, and a spiky tail. It had 13 pairs of legs but was probably a swimmer because the legs were veiled by large gill lobes. *Leanchoilia's* most unusual feature was a pair of long, whiplike appendages extending forward from the base of the head. These appendages were jointed about halfway along their length, like a bullwhip. Three lashes extended from the base of each appendage. These appendages were probably stretched out in front of *Lean-choilia* to find and gather food. They also could be tucked under the creature's body when it was at rest on the seafloor.

Measuring only one to two inches (2.5 to 5 cm), *Wiwaxia* was a small creature but ranks large as one of the enigmas of the Burgess organisms. *Wiwaxia* had a body plan like no other known animal. It was covered by a protective shell made up of smaller, overlapping plates. From the side, *Wiwaxia* was shaped like half a walnut shell. The makeup of the plates resembled the thatching of a tiny, woven straw hat. In addition to the plates, *Wiwaxia* had two fantastic rows of long spines sticking up along its middle, probably to protect it from predators. Underneath its imposing protective shell were the soft parts and legs that it used to moved along the bottom of the sea. One *Wiwaxia* specimen had a tiny, shelled brachiopod attached to its back. This evidence suggests that *Wiwaxia* did not burrow into the sediment because the brachiopod could not have survived if it had. *Wiwaxia's* jaws were at its rear, presumably to collect food particles swept back by its legs as *Wiwaxia* crawled along the bottom sediment.

The onychophorans, or velvet worms, are rare creatures found today in the Southern Hemisphere. They live in hiding in modern tropical forests, but their ancestral roots are represented in the fossils of the Burgess Shale by one of the strangest creatures of all, *Hallucigenia*. Its name alone, meaning dreamlike creature, hints at the puzzle that has faced the scientists who have tried to decipher its body plan. *Hallucigenia* was only 1.25 inches (3 cm) long. Fossils of *Hallucigenia* are as flat as a pancake, revealing a tubular body like a worm, a blob for a possible head, an open tube for a possible rear end, and an assortment of spikes and tentacles attached to one side or the other of the body.

The puzzle of *Hallucigenia* has always been to try to know which end was up. Without eyes or a recognizable mouth, without an obvious front or rear end, which side of *Hallucigenia* was up? A well-known reconstruction in 1977 had the animal walking on seven pairs of spiky stilts. These "legs" were not jointed, making the mobility of the animal difficult to imagine. On top of the tube-shaped body was a single row of seven long tentacles, each with a pronged tip. One theory suggested that the end of each tentacle was actually a separate mouth. This was not so far-fetched, given that no other kind of mouth was visible. Nor were the tentacles long enough to reach the bulbous end of the animal, which was presumed to be the head and the natural place for a mouth. *Hallucigenia* thus was pictured as a stilt-walking worm with seven tentacle-mounted mouths.

This image of *Hallucigenia* stuck until 1992, when, on reexamination of the original specimen, a second "tentacle" leg row was discovered. This evidence, in addition to the discovery of a similar specimen in Early Cambrian fossil deposits in China, once again turned *Hallucigenia* upside down. Now it was walking on its "tentacle" legs, with the seven pairs of spikes on its back for protection. The mysterious bulbous head was also removed from the new interpretation, as it now was presumed to be a stain in the Burgess specimens and not a body part.

Odontogriphus was, until recently, a little-understood creature originally thought to be a suspension feeder. For many years *Odontogriphus* was known only from one important specimen represented on two facing slabs of shale; the top of the animal was on one slab, and the bottom was on the other. But even telling top from bottom was not easy. *Odontogriphus* appeared to be little more than a soft, flattened blob about 2½ inches (8 cm) long. A new description of *Odontogriphus* published in 2006 and based on 189 new specimens revealed much more about the creature. *Odontogriphus* was a flat, oval-shaped creature with an average size of 1.9 inches (4.75 cm), the largest known specimen being 4.9 inches (12.5 cm). The underside of the body's perimeter was lined with tiny ctenidia, small bud-like appendages that assisted the animal in breathing. Near one end of the underside was a small mouth lined with rows of chevron-shaped teeth. It appears that *Odontogriphus* used its teeth to scrape off bits of living algae from the abundant algae mats that covered the bottom of its habitat.

Suspension Feeders

Some of the animals of the Burgess Shale have the uncanny appearance of plants. An example is *Thaumaptilon*, a featherlike escapee from the Vendian extinction in the Precambrian. Standing eight inches (10 cm) tall, it was large by Middle Cambrian standards. *Thaumaptilon* had a long central stem to which a series of branch-like limbs were attached. These branches were covered by a ribbed membrane resembling the underside of a mushroom cap. The other side of this membrane was smooth. *Thaumaptilon* had a holdfast to keep it anchored, and probably remained stationary most of the time. *Thaumaptilon* fed by catching food particles from the water that flowed into its featherlike structure. The somewhat quilted appearance of *Thaumaptilon* suggests that it might be related to the diverse group of Vendian quilted creatures. In its Burgess Shale form, *Thaumaptilon* is considered an ancestor of the modern sea pen. With a little imagination, one can picture a seafloor covered by a slowly undulating and moving forest of these passively feeding creatures.

Another animal with links to the present was *Choia*, an ancestral sponge. It was only about one inch (2.5 cm) in diameter and resembled a straw hat that has been flattened by a steam roller. *Choia* laid flat on the seafloor and had many spines that radiated out from its center. The spines probably helped *Choia* collect and filter food particles from the water. Its food consisted of bacteria, algae, and other small organic particles in the water. The spines may also have transported trapped food particles to *Choia's* digestive cells.

Of the ancestral forms of life found in the Burgess Shale, one small, ribbonlike creature holds a special place in the history of animals with backbones. *Pikaia*, a tiny, 1½-inch (4 cm) long animal was not a vertebrate, but it was an early form of life that led to the evolution of animals with backbones. A member of the phylum Chordata, *Pikaia* had a notochord, a long, stiffening rod that runs the length of a body and supports the animal's nerve cord. In *Pikaia*, the notochord served as the framework for its flexible, ribbonlike form. Attached to the notochord were bands of muscles to help power the free-swimming creature. *Pikaia* most likely fed in the same manner as known species of modern chordates such as the lancet, using its mouth to take in water as it swam, filtering out food particles, and then passing the water back out through its gills.

Although one cannot say for sure that *Pikaia* was a direct ancestor of the vertebrates, let alone of humans, it certainly possessed the kinds of traits that eventually led to the evolution of animals with backbones. *Pikaia* is a tantalizing connection between the weird and wonderful creatures of the Burgess Shale and animals of the present day. Since the discovery of *Pikaia*, several new—and even earlier—fossils of chordates have been discovered in China, including *Haikouella, Yunnanozoon,* and the much-celebrated *Myllokunmingia* and *Haikouichthys,* now considered the earliest known animals with a backbone. Along with *Pikaia*, they are the earliest known clue to the origin of vertebrates.

Predators and Scavengers

Although there are no living trilobites today, they were common members of the ocean fauna from 275 million to 500 million years ago. They have roots in the Early Cambrian, and they spread rapidly throughout the Middle and Late Cambrian. More than 4,000 species are known from the fossil record, an incredible number for an extinct creature. What is a trilobite? The name trilobite means "three-part body," which is part of what makes these creatures a particular kind of arthropod. A trilobite's body was made up of three parts—the head, the middle, and the rear. Each part was protected by a hard shield. Furthermore, the middle of the body was divided into seven jointed parts. Trilobites had jointed legs, and most walked on the seafloor. They ranged in length from only a few millimeters to 27 inches (70 cm). The armored head area had two antennae and a pair of multifaceted eyes similar to those of king crabs.

While some trilobites are thought to have been swimmers, most lived on the seafloor. As active scavengers or predators, trilobites used tiny spines at the base of their legs to shuffle prey or food

(continues on page 190)

THINK ABOUT IT

Ninety-Five Years of Misidentification: The Case of *Anomalocaris*

The scientific process can result in mistakes. Good science emphasizes a continuing process of detecting errors in existing information and making corrections. This process is common in the field of paleontology because the first discovered example of a fossil specimen may not be as good as finds that follow. Each new find sheds additional light on the original fossil, allowing details to become clearer and helping science to correct itself along the way.

The Burgess Shale fauna have included many cases of mistaken identify. This is partly because animals found in Middle Cambrian fossil beds are so unlike animals recognized today. It is as if one were to explore an alien planet where the biology was totally unknown. In fact, considering how far removed in time the Cambrian Period is from today, this comparison is nearly true.

One case in point is one of the largest known Cambrian predators, the fierce-looking *Anomalocaris*. One of the first predators with jawlike structures, it was about two feet (60 cm) long. The body of *Anomalocaris* was long and glided slowly across the bottom of the ocean by the power of segmented flaps on its sides and a tail with two fins. The creature's mouth was on the underside of its head. *Anomalocaris* was made of a segmented circle of plates that could constrict to crush its prey. It shoveled food into its mouth by means of two coiling arms that reached out just in front of it as it swam.

This amazing creature was part of one of most intriguing mysteries of the Burgess Shale. Before 1985, nobody had ever found or recognized a complete specimen of *Anomalocaris*. In 1886, its name had been given to a partial specimen that consisted of one of the front feeding appendages. In isolation, that appendage looked something like a shrimp, and the name it was given means "odd shrimp." That is what *Anomalocaris* was thought to be for nearly a hundred years. In the meantime, among the dozens of bizarre creatures named from the Burgess Shale, Walcott also named two other curious creatures that figure in this tale. One was

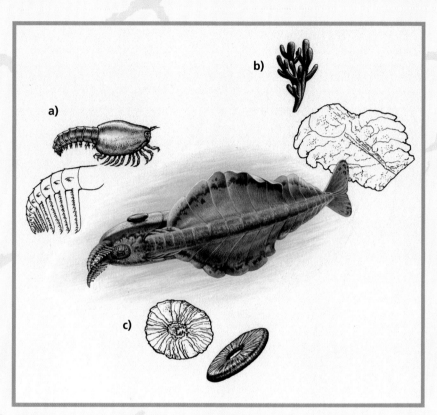

One case of mistaken identity in the Burgess Shale took 95 years to solve: The large Cambrian predator *Anomalocaris* was unknown until 1985. Prior to that, several isolated parts of the creature were misidentified as species of their own. These included a feeding arm originally given the name *Anomalocaris* (a); the sponge-like *Laggania* which turned out to be its body (b); and the swimming disc-like *Peytoia*, which was actually the mouth of *Anomalocaris* (c).

Laggania (1911), a large, flat-bodied fossil thought to be a kind of sponge. The other was *Peytoia* (1911), a small disc that looked like a pineapple ring, with 32 lobes around a circular opening in the middle. Walcott thought

(continues)

(continued)

that *Peytoia* was probably part of a jellyfish, although no known jellyfish had an appendage such as this.

Walcott's view of these four individual creatures—*Anomalocaris, Laggania,* and *Peytoia*—held until the 1980s. Until about 1980, illustrations in popular books and magazines still pictured *Anomalocaris* as an armorplated shrimp with a prickly tail, and *Peytoia* as a sort of living Frisbee navigating the ancient waters.

The true picture of *Anomalocaris* became apparent because of the work of paleontologists Derek Briggs (b. 1950) and Harry Whittington (b. 1916). In 1981, while examining several blocks of Burgess Shale fossils, they discovered specimens of these four fossil creatures in association with one another. It soon became apparent that *Laggania* was the body of *Anomalocaris, Peytoia* was its mouth, and the original specimen named *Anomalocaris* was actually one of a pair of its feeding arms.

After many decades of misinterpretation, the true picture of *Anomalocaris* took shape, and the creature emerged as the largest and most fearsome-looking predator of the Canadian Cambrian fauna.

(continued from page 187)

particles to the mouth, which was located on the underside of the head. One of their favorite foods may have been marine worms living in the sediment. Trilobites probably could burrow into the sediment, and some species could roll up their bodies for protection, like modern pill bugs. Most trilobites are known only from fossils of their molted exoskeletons, the hard outer coverings that were shed as the animals grew. Some remarkable specimens of whole trilobites, however, show some of the soft parts, legs, antennae, and other features that reveal how these creatures probably lived. Several early species of trilobites are found in the Burgess Shale, including

Olenoides and *Naraoia*. The latter retained some primitive traits such as two rather than three body shields.

Anomalocaris was the biggest, and probably the fiercest, predator of the Burgess Shale fauna. One of the first predators with a jawlike structure, the Burgess Shale *Anomalocaris* was about two feet (60 cm) long. A related species found in China was a whopping six feet (1.8 m) long. This early arthropod appears to have been an active stalker, hovering over the bottom of the ocean and looking for prey all the time.

Not all Cambrian predators were as large and fearsome as *Anomalocaris*. *Aysheaia* was a two-inch (5 cm) creature that was probably an ancestor of today's velvet worms. It looked a little like a corrugated rubber hose. On its underside, *Aysheaia* had 10 pairs of conelike legs. The legs were not composed of articulated segments like those of arthropods; they had no joints and did not bend. The legs, however, were tipped by tiny claws to aid *Aysheaia* in getting a grip. The head end of the creature had a small round hole, presumably a mouth, surrounded by six spinelike appendages. This arrangement made the head end of *Aysheaia* look something like the socket end of a fluorescent light bulb. *Aysheaia* also had two appendages on either side of its head. Each appendage was tipped with three branchlike fingers. These may have helped *Aysheaia* fasten itself to its prey. What did this little predator eat? Many remains of *Aysheaia* have been found among fossils of coral, so it is reasonable to presume that this slow-moving animal was feeding on them. *Aysheaia*'s stumpy legs and gripping claws probably kept it fastened as it climbed along, eating its way over the coral.

Another Middle Cambrian creature that was an early arthropod was *Sidneyia*. The first specimen was found by Charles Walcott's son, after whom he named it. Its full name is *Sidneyia inexpectans*, or "Sidney's surprise." Even though it was only two to five inches (5 to 13 cm) long, *Sidneyia* was one of the largest predators found in the Burgess Shale. It fed on small crustaceans and trilobites. *Sidneyia* had an armored head, an oval-shaped body covering, and a plated tail. Its legs and gills were tucked neatly underneath its top shell. The shell itself appeared to be constructed of nine overlapping bands, with corresponding pairs of legs and gills underneath.

Sidneyia's legs grabbed and pushed tiny animals and morsels of food to its mouth. One specimen of *Sidneyia* included a tiny trilobite in its digestive track, indicating what might have been its last meal.

Opabinia is another Burgess Shale creature that defies definition. Although it looks a little like a shrimp or maybe even a lobster, it lacks some of the features, such as legs, that would place it in this group. *Opabinia* does not belong to any known surviving phyla of animals. Measuring only three inches (7.5 cm) long, *Opabinia* was a tiny monster. It had five bulging eyes, the likes of which seem to appear only in science fiction. It had a tube-shaped body with 15 segments, each with a pair of lobes on the sides. These gave *Opabinia* a pulsating means of moving about, like a tiny version of the fleshy wings of a manta ray. All but two of the lobes had a frilly gill on their topside.

Opabinia may have swum freely, or it may have fluttered across the sediment on the seafloor. Attached to its bulbous head was a long appendage unlike those normally found on arthropods. This appendage made up one-third of the length of the animal. This single hoselike appendage had a kind of pincer on its tip, with a set of tiny spines. The appendage was bendable. *Opadinia* probably captured small prey in its pincers and then shoveled the prey into its mouth. Its tail had three additional pairs of lobes that presumably helped it swim. As for eating habits, *Opabinia* may have thrust its pincers into the mud to capture worms and other small prey.

SUMMARY

This chapter explored the organisms of the Cambrian Period, their relationship to today's life, and how the discovery of the Cambrian fauna has influenced thinking about evolution.

1. The warming of the climate at the end of the Precambrian Period melted glaciers and flooded the world with mineral-rich waters.
2. By the end of the Cambrian Period (488 million years ago), the super continent Gondwana had formed.

3. The most common life-forms in the Early Cambrian were the small shelly faunas, archaeocyathids, and other creatures of which only slight traces are available.

4. The Middle Cambrian experienced an explosion of new life-forms.

5. Most of the 23 modern phyla of animals have roots in the Middle Cambrian.

6. Important sites of Cambrian fossils include the Burgess Shale, in British Columbia, Canada; Chengjiang, in Yunnan Province, China; and Sirius Passet, on the northern coast of Greenland.

7. The animals of the Burgess Shale evolved during a geologically short span of time—about 15 million years.

8. Species appear capable of evolving rapidly and spectacularly when new habitats appear.

9. Rapid evolution has happened more than once in Earth's past.

10. Today's animal phyla with roots in the Cambrian Period include arthropods, annelids, onychophorans, chordates, poriferans, cnidarians, priopulids, and sipunculans.

11. Most of the Burgess Shale creatures fall into one of three categories of lifestyles that are still seen in ocean creatures today: deposit feeders; suspension feeders; and predators and scavengers.

12. Early chordates were one of the taxa that survived the Cambrian-Ordovician mass extinction, thereby leading to the evolution of vertebrates.

CONCLUSION

The end of the Cambrian Period witnessed violent shifts in Earth's tectonic plates and widespread volcanic eruptions. These geologic occurrences caused a gradual drop in the level of the sea. Over many hundreds of years, this change transformed the shallow-water habitats occupied by some of the most plentiful and wondrous Cambrian creatures. While many phyla of animals adapted successfully to the changing conditions, nearly half (42 percent) could not and so became extinct. The drop in the level of the sea brought the end of a way of life that had reigned supreme in Earth's oceans for many millions of years.

It is fitting that this book closes with the Cambrian Period because it was truly the gateway to the future of all other organisms on the planet. Those phyla that survived the Cambrian-Ordovician extinction began a comeback that took them into the open oceans and eventually onto land.

Among the select kinds of animals that squeaked through the Cambrian-Ordovician mass extinction were the early chordates. The early chordates are represented in the Cambrian period by *Pikaia* from Canada and *Haikouella, Haikouichthys, Yunnanozoon,* and *Myllokunmingia* from China. If ever there was a taxa that seemed least likely to succeed, it was the chordates. In a world dominated by armor-plated arthropods and free-swimming predators with vicious claws and jaws, the early chordates were remarkable because of their conspicuous lack of protection. The secret of their early survival is unknown, but the fact that early chordates were probably agile swimmers would have

Cambrian Life

enabled them to elude predators and remain mobile in the open ocean even as gradual changes in sea level radically changed near-shore habitats.

The survival and evolution of the chordates would figure greatly in the future of the planet. The early chordates soon evolved into fishes, the first dominant form of vertebrate to occupy the oceans. From the fishes came backboned creatures that eventually migrated onto land, thereby leading to the development of amphibians, reptiles, dinosaurs, mammals, and birds. As time went on, the early vertebrates conquered both the sea and the land.

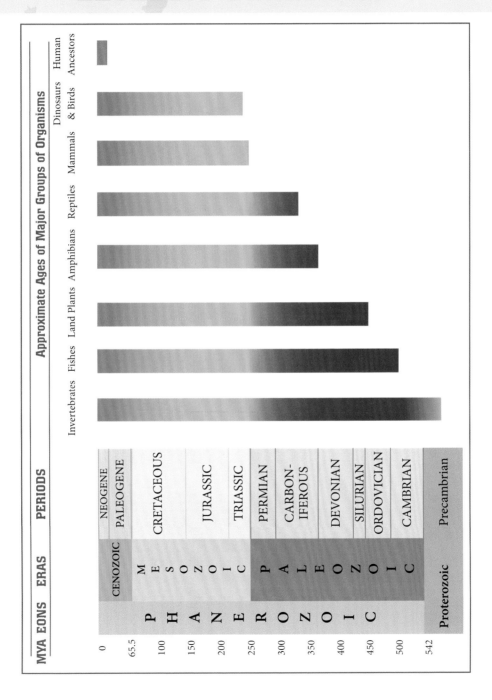

APPENDIX B:
ANATOMICAL DIRECTIONS

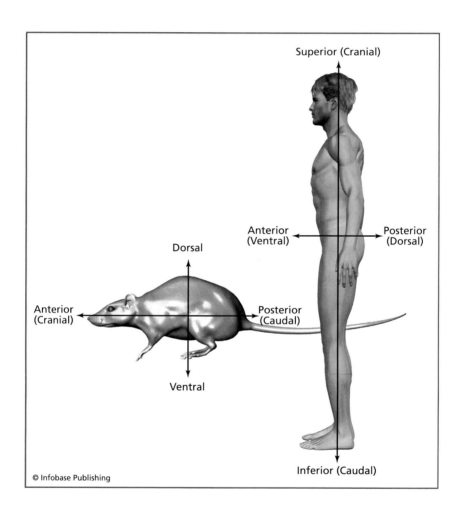

GLOSSARY

absolute dating   A technique for determining the age of a rock by measuring the rates of decay of radioactive elements found in the rock; also called radiometric dating.

adaptation   Change made by an organism in response to environmental stress.

analogies   Similar inherited traits that arise in organisms that are not related to one another.

anatomy   Term used to describe the basic biological systems of an animal, such as the skeletal and muscular systems.

annelids   (Annelida) Animal phylum whose members have a fluid-filled, segmented body, are worm-shaped, have a nervous system on the underside of the body, and possess at least one pair of hairlike bristles; annelids include worms that live on the land and in the sea, and leeches.

Archaea   One of the three domains of living organisms; it includes members of the kingdom Archaebacteria—single-celled organisms whose cells do not have a nucleus (prokaryotes) and whose metabolism is not oxygen-based (anaerobic).

archaebacteria   Members of the domain Archaea, these prokaryotic microbes are single-celled organisms whose cells do not have a nucleus (prokaryotes) and whose metabolism is not oxygen-based (anaerobic).

arthropods   (Arthropoda) Animal phylum whose members have a segmented body, body regions dedicated to specific functions, a jointed exoskeleton, and a nervous system on the underside of the body; arthropods include trilobites, crabs, lobsters, brine shrimp, barnacles, insects, spiders, scorpions, and centipedes.

background extinction   A background extinction may occur suddenly, or it may occur slowly, over a long period of time; a background extinction usually affect only one species at a time.

Bacteria   One of the three domains of living organisms; it includes members of the kingdom Bacteria—single-celled organisms whose cells do not have a nucleus (prokaryotes) and whose metabolism is oxygen-based.

bias   Word used to describe natural circumstances that favor fossilization, including the population, anatomy, size, and biology and habitat of a species.

big bang   An enormous explosion of cosmic matter that formed the universe; the big bang was so powerful that the universe is still expanding today because of it.

Cambrian Period   Period of geologic time lasting from 488 million to 542 million years ago.

carbon-14 dating   A form of absolute dating based on the decay rate of the element carbon 14, which is taken in by living organisms from the air; once an animal dies, carbon 14 begins to decay.

cast   A type of fossil made when a body mold from an organism is filled with another element; a cast can retain the outer shape and size of the organism.

chordates   (Chordata) Animal phylum whose members possess a notochord, a nerve cord that runs on top of the notochord, and gill slits for breathing; chordates include lancelets, salps, ascidians, and larvaceans.

cladistics   A way of classifying organisms by comparing their anatomical features; categorizing groups of organisms because of their shared characteristics.

cladogram   A diagram used to illustrate the cladistic (evolutionary) relationships between groups of organisms.

climate   The kind of weather that occurs at a particular place over time.

cnidarians   (Cnidaria) Animal phylum whose members have a body consisting of a large central chamber that receives and digests food; includes corals, jellyfish, sea anemones, sea fans, sea pens, and the Portuguese man-of-war.

continental drift   The slow and gradual movement and transformation of the continents due to shifting of the tectonic plates of Earth's crust.

convection   Circulation of liquid or gaseous material due to changing temperatures.

convergent evolution   Term used to describe a situation in which unrelated species each develop similar adaptations to similar environmental conditions.

coprolite   Fossilized animal feces.

core   A region at the center of the Earth; the core consists of a dense, solid inner core, at the center of the Earth, that floats within a surrounding liquid outer core.

cross-cutting The principle of cross-cutting states that any geologic feature is younger than anything else that it cuts across.

crust The outer layer of the Earth, including both dry land and ocean floors.

deposit feeder Marine animal that eats by extracting nutrients from mud on the seafloor.

developmental Pertaining to aspects of the reproduction and growth of organisms.

DNA (deoxyribonucleic acid) The molecule of life, which carries genetic instructions from parent to offspring.

domain A taxonomic level of classification higher than the kingdom; the domain was proposed in the 1970s by Carl Woese and George Fox but not widely accepted until 1996; the three domains of life are Bacteria, Archaea, and Eukarya.

ecosystem A populations of living organisms and the environment in which they live.

endoskeleton An internal skeleton, usually consisting of bones, such as is found in vertebrates.

eon The three longest spans of geologic time; the Archean ("ancient") Eon stretched from the earliest Earth, 4.5 billion years ago, to 2.5 billion years ago; the Proterozoic ("early life") Eon began after the Archean and lasted from 2.5 billion to 542 million years ago; the Phanerozoic ("visible life") Eon began 542 million years ago and still goes on.

epicenter The location on Earth's surface directly above the point of origin of an earthquake.

era A span of geologic time ranking below the eon; the Archean Eon is divided into four eras dating from more than 4 billion years ago to 2.5 billion years ago; the Proterozoic Eon is divided into three eras dating from 2.5 billion years ago to about 542 million years ago; the ongoing Phanerozoic Eon is divided into three eras, the Paleozoic, the Mesozoic, and the Cenozoic; the Paleozoic ("ancient life") Era lasted from 542 million to 251 million years ago; the Mesozoic ("middle life") Era lasted from 251 million to 65 million years ago; the Cenozoic ("recent life") Era began 65 million years ago and continues to the present.

erosion The removal and displacement of Earth's surface by the action of running water, rain, wind, glaciers and ice sheets.

Eukarya One of the three domains of living organisms; it includes four kingdoms—Protista, Fungi, Plantae, and Animalia—all of which consist of multicelled organisms with a distinct cell structure whose nucleus contains strands of DNA.

eukaryotes   Living organisms in the domain Eukarya; multicelled organisms with a distinct cell structure whose nucleus contains strands of DNA.

evaporate   To turn water into gas by heating it; sunlight evaporates water from oceans, lakes, and streams.

evolution   The natural process that causes species to change gradually over time; evolution is controlled by changes to the genetic code—the DNA—of organisms.

exoskeleton   A skeleton that forms on the outside of the body, as in invertebrates such as arthropods.

extinction   The irreversible elimination of an entire species of plant or animal because the species cannot adapt effectively to changes in its environment.

fauna   Animals found in a given ecosystem.

forelimb   One of the two front legs of a vertebrate

fossil   Any physical trace of prehistoric life.

fossilization   The physical process by which the remains of an organism become a fossil.

gene   A microscopic unit on a DNA molecule that controls inherited traits.

genetics   The scientific study of DNA, genes, and inherited traits.

geologic timescale   A scale for measuring time based on observations about the layers of the Earth and how long these layers took to accumulate.

geophysics   A branch of geology that studies the composition and structure of Earth, its atmosphere, its oceans, and its magnetic fields based on the principles of physics.

gradualism   Evolution through slow and gradual changes over a long period of time that lead to major biological changes to a species.

gravity meter   A scientific instrument that measures small fractions of the gravitational attraction between the Earth and a mass within the instrument.

hind limb   One of the two rear legs of a vertebrate.

homeostasis   The natural biological stability of a living organism.

homologies   Structural and behavioral traits that different species of organisms have inherited from a common ancestor.

hybrid   An offspring of two animals of different varieties, breeds, or species, such as a mule.

igneous rock   Rock that forms from the cooling of once-molten matter from the interior of the Earth.

impact crater   A crater in the crust of the Earth caused by the strike of an extraterrestrial body such as an asteroid or meteorite.

kingdom   One of the six major hierarchical classifications of life at a taxonomic level just under domain; the six kingdoms are Archaebacteria, Bacteria, Protista, Fungi, Plantae, and Animalia.

lobopodia   A proposed new phylum of invertebrates that includes two classes, the extinct Xenusia for marine forms, and Onychophora, now a phylum, for terrestrial forms such as velvet worms.

long-term biological adaptation   A physiological change that occurs when an organism acclimates to long-term exposure to a new or changing environment; long-term biological adaptations are not passed on to offspring.

magma   Hot, liquid rock in Earth's mantle and crust; called lava when it comes to the surface through a volcanic eruption.

magnetometer   A scientific instrument that measures the strength of Earth's magnetic field.

mantle   A layer of the Earth that surrounds the core and lies between the core and the outer surface or crust.

mass extinction   An extinction event that kills off more than 25 percent of all species in a million years or less.

metabolism   The ability of a living organism to get energy and nutrients from the outside, convert outside energy and nutrients into its own energy, release waste, and grow.

metazoans   Multicelled organisms.

mineralization   A process of fossilization caused by water seepage through a layer of earth containing the remains of an organism; over time, minerals carried by the water replace parts of the organism's bone with stone.

mold   A type of fossil created when the body of an organism dissolves away, leaving a hollow impression of an original body part in the sedimentary rock.

molecular   Consisting of molecules; pertaining to the microscopic study of biological molecules.

molecular cladistics   In the classifying of organisms, a discipline that compares biological elements of different species at the molecular level; this discipline includes the study of genes and DNA.

morphological   Pertaining to the body form and structure of an organism.

mutations   Slight, unpredictable variations in the genetic code that happen when organisms reproduce.

natural selection   One of Charles Darwin's observations regarding the way evolution works; given the complex and changing conditions under which life exists, those individuals with the most favorable combination of inherited traits may survive and reproduce while others may not.

notochord   A stiff rod running along the back of an organism; found in members of the phylum Chordata.

oceanic ridge   Undersea mountain range.

onychophorans   (Onychophora) Animal phylum whose members possess 14 to 43 pairs of unjointed legs, a worm-shaped body, two antennae, appendages forming jaws around the mouth, and two more stubby appendages near the mouth; onychophorans include the velvet and "walking" worms.

organism   Any living plant, animal, bacterium, archaebacterium, protist, or fungus.

paleontologist   A scientist who studies prehistoric life, often using fossils.

period   A span of geologic time ranking below the era; the Phanerozoic Eon is divided into three eras and 11 periods, each covering a span of millions of years; the longest of these periods, including the three in the Mesozoic Era, are sometimes further broken down into smaller divisions of time.

photosynthesis   A metabolic process in which an organism's cells convert energy from the Sun, carbon dioxide, and water to reproduce their cells; the waste product of photosynthesis is free oxygen released into the atmosphere.

phyla   The major subdivisions of organisms after one of the three major kingdoms of life; the word *phyla* is the plural of *phylum.*

phylogeny   The history of the evolutionary relationships among species, which can be diagrammed; also known as the tree of life.

physiology   The way in which an animal's parts work together and are adapted to help the organism survive.

population   Members of the same species that live in a particular area.

poriferans   (Porifera) Animal phylum whose members have cells that are not organized into tissues or organs; poriferans are composed primarily of chambers for channeling water; they include the sponges.

Precambrian   The unit of geologic time that lasted from the beginning of the Earth, 4.5 billion years ago, until 542 million years ago.

precipitation   Rain or snow.

predation   Feeding on other live animals.

predator   An animal that actively seeks and feeds on other live animals.

prehistory   History of life on Earth prior to the written history of humans; prehistoric time.

priapulids   (Priapulida) Animal phylum whose members have unsegmented, tubular bodies; members of this phylum include carnivorous worms.

prokaryotes   Single-celled organisms whose cells do not have a nucleus; the prokaryotes include members of the domains Archaea and Bacteria.

punctuated equilibria   Rapid evolution of a given species due to a rapid change in its habitat; after such a crisis, a short period of rapid evolution may take place that affects a subset of a species population.

relative dating   Determining the date of one layer of the Earth by comparing it to a previously identified layer.

rift   In Earth's crust, a gap between two tectonic plates that have moved apart.

scavenger   An animal that feeds on the dead remains of other animals.

sedimentary rock   Rock that forms in layers from the debris of other rocks or the remains of organisms.

seismic reflection   The return of seismic waves to the Earth's surface after they have bounced off a rock boundary in the Earth's interior.

seismic refraction   The bending of seismic waves as they pass through rock boundaries of varying composition and thickness.

seismograph   A scientific instrument used to detect, measure, and record seismic waves caused by earthquakes, thereby creating a permanent record of Earth's motion.

self-organization   A mathematical basis for predicting the seemingly spontaneous occurrence of order, developed by Stuart Kauffman as an adjunct to the evolutionary theory of natural selection.

short-term biological adaptation   A temporary physiological change that occurs naturally in an organism when it encounters a change to its environment; short-term biological adaptations are not passed on to offspring.

sipunculans   (Sipuncula) Animal phylum whose members have a plump, peanut-shaped, unsegmented body with a long mouth appendage that can be retracted into the body; sipunculans' bodies are muscular, with a hard outer covering; they include burrowing marine worms.

small shelly fauna   Tiny marine animals from the Early Cambrian Period whose remains include fossils of the hard, shell-like body parts they left behind.

species   In classification, the most basic biological unit of living organisms; members of a species can interbreed and produce fertile offspring.

stromatolites   Near-shore, mutilayered, rocklike structures created by photosynthesizing bacterial organisms that live in vast colonies in shallow ocean waters; fossil stromatolites represent one of the oldest known records of life.

subduction zone   A deep trench in the seafloor caused by the collision of tectonic plates.

superposition   The principle of superposition states that younger sedimentary rocks are deposited on top of older sedimentary rocks.

suspension feeding   Marine animal that catches, traps, and filters out food particles floating through the water.

taxon   In classification, a single kind of organism.

taxa   In classification, a group of related organisms.

taxonomy   The science of classifying living and extinct species of organisms.

tectonic plates   Large, slowly moving slabs of crust that ride on top of Earth's semiliquid and molten mantle.

tetrapods   Vertebrate animals with four legs and two-legged and legless vertebrates descended from them; tetrapods include amphibians, reptiles, mammals, and birds.

trace fossil   A type of fossil that preserves evidence of the presence of a prehistoric organism but that does not include body parts; fossilized trackways or feces are examples of trace fossils.

trackway   The fossilized footprints or markings left by a prehistoric animal.

transitional fossil   A fossil that represents one step in the many stages that exist as a species evolves.

trilobite   An extinct form of arthropod whose fossils are found in rocks dating from the Early Cambrian to the Late Permian Periods; trilobites had a three-part body and a hard exoskeleton.

uniformitarianism   A geologic principle originating with James Hutton; it states that the geologic forces that can be observed in the present are the same as the forces that shaped the Earth in the past.

Vendian   Name assigned to a division of time, from 542 million to 630 million years ago, during which some of the earliest forms of multicelled animals lived.

Vendian fauna   Multicelled animals that lived during Vendian times, from 541 million to 630 million years ago.

viruses   Biological entities whose members consist of fragments of genetic material that become activated and reproduce when in contact with the cell of another organism; because viruses cannot reproduce by themselves, they are technically not considered to be alive.

CHAPTER BIBLIOGRAPHY

Introduction

Wilford, John Noble. "When No One Read, Who Started to Write?" *The New York Times* (April, 6, 1999). Available online. URL: http://query.nytimes.com/gst/fullpage.html?res=9B01EFD61139F935A35757C0A96F958260. Accessed October 8, 2007.

Chapter 1 – The Changing Earth

Kious, W. Jacquelyne, and Robert I. Tilling. *This Dynamic Earth: The Story of Plate Tectonics.* Washington, DC: The United States Geologic Survey, 2001.

Kottak, Conrad Phillip. *Anthropology: The Exploration of Human Diversity.* New York: McGraw-Hill, 2004.

Palmer, Douglas. *Atlas of the Prehistoric World.* New York: Discovery Books, 1999.

Plummer, Charles C., David McGeary, and Diane H. Carlson. *Physical Geology.* New York: McGraw-Hill, 2005.

Prothero, Donald R., and Robert H. Dott Jr. *Evolution of the Earth.* New York: McGraw-Hill, 2004.

Russell, Dale A. *An Odyssey In Time: The Dinosaurs of North America.* Minocqua, WI: North Word Press, 1989.

United States Geologic Survey. "Inside the Earth," Available online. URL: http://pubs.usgs.gov/publications/text/inside.html. Accessed October 8, 2007.

University of California Museum of Paleontology. "Plate Tectonics: The Mechanism." Available online. URL: http://www.ucmp.berkeley.edu/geology/tecmech.html. Accessed October 8, 2007.

Chapter 2 – Geologic Time

The International Commission on Stratigraphy. "International Stratigraphic Chart" ["Time Scale Chart"]. Available online. URL: http://www.stratigraphy.org/. Accessed October 8, 2007.

Kottak, Conrad Phillip. *Physical Anthropology and Archaeology*. New York: McGraw-Hill, 2004.

McKinney, Frank. "Determining Age of Rocks and Fossils." The Museum of Paleontology of The University of California and The Paleontological Society. Available online. URL: http://www.ucmp. berkeley.edu/fosrec/McKinney.html. Accessed October 8, 2007.

Norman, David. *Prehistoric Life: The Rise of the Vertebrates*. New York: Macmillan, 1994.

Relethford, John, H. *The Human Species: An Introduction to Biological Anthropology*. Mountain View, CA: Mayfield Publishing, 2000.

Chapter 3 – Fossils: Clues to Past Life

Bebout, John W. "What Percentage of All Livings Things Eventually Becomes Fossilized?" Washington University Medical School, 2004. Available online. URL: http://www.madsci.org/posts/archives/ aug97/871343510.Ev.r.html. Accessed October 8, 2007.

Dunbar, Carl O., and Karl M. Waage. *Historical Geology, Third Edition*. New York: John Wiley & Sons, 1969.

Khamsi, Roxanne. "Ancient Mammal Genes Reconstructed." *Nature News*, December 1, 2004. Available online. URL: http://www. bioedonline.org/news/news.cfm?art=1418. Accessed October 8, 2007.

Lucas, Spencer G. *Dinosaurs: The Textbook, Fourth Edition*. New York: McGraw-Hill, 2004.

Platt, Garry. "Dinosaurs from Amber?" Available online. URL: http:// www.gplatt.demon.co.uk/amberdna.htm. Accessed October 8, 2007.

Plummer, Charles C., David McGeary, and Diane H. Carlson. *Physical Geology*. New York: McGraw-Hill, 2005.

Prothero, Donald R., and Robert H. Dott Jr. *Evolution of the Earth*. New York: McGraw-Hill, 2004.

Chapter 4 – Extinction

Dunbar, Carl O., and Karl M. Waage. *Historical Geology, Third Edition*. New York: John Wiley & Sons, 1969.

Ellis, Richard. *No Turning Back: The Life and Death of Animal Species*. New York: Harper Collins, 2004.

Surovell, Todd, Nicole Waguespack, and P. Jeffrey Brantingham. "Global Archaeological Evidence For Proboscidean Overkill, Proceedings of the National Academy of Sciences." Available online. URL: http://www. pnas.org/cgi/content/full/102/17/6231. Accessed October 8, 2007.

Chapter 5 – Life and Evolution

American Society for Microbiology. "Bacteria." Microbeworld. Available online. URL: http://www.microbeworld.org/microbes/bacteria/. Accessed October 8, 2007.

Benton, M.J., V.P. Tverdokhlebov, and M.V. Surkov. "Ecosystem Remodeling Among Vertebrates at the Permian-Triassic Boundary in Russia." *Nature,* Vol. 432, (November 4, 2004): 97.

Coombs, Jennifer. "Mass Extinctions—Definition and Causes." Northeastern University. Available online. URL: www.casdn.neu.edu/~geology/department/staff/coombs/class_notes/1141/1141-23.htm. Accessed February 21, 2005.

Edey, Maitland A., and Donald C. Johanson. *Blueprints: Solving the Mystery of Evolution.* Boston: Little, Brown, 1989.

Eldredge, Niles. *Time Frames: The Rethinking of Darwinian Evolution and the Theory of Punctuated Equilibria.* New York: Simon and Schuster, 1985.

Feder, Kenneth L. *The Past in Perspective.* New York, McGraw-Hill, 2004.

Fortey, Richard. *Life: A Natural History of the First Four Billion Years of Life on Earth.* New York: Alfred A. Knopf, 1998.

Gardom, Tim, and Angela Milner. *The Book of Dinosaurs.* Rocklin, CA: Prima Publishing, 1993.

Khamsi, Roxanne. "Ancient Mammal Genes Reconstructed." *Nature News*, December 1, 2004. Available online. URL: http://www.bioedonline.org/news/news.cfm?art=1418. Accessed October 8, 2007.

Kottak, Conrad Phillip. *Physical Anthropology and Archaeology.* New York: McGraw-Hill, 2004.

Mayell, Hillary, "Three High-Altitude Peoples, Three Adaptations to Thin Air." *National Geographic News.* Available online. URL: http://news.nationalgeographic.com/news/2004/02/0224_040225_evolution.html. Accessed October 8, 2007.

McKie, Robin. "Neanderthal Man Type Site Rediscovered." *Japan Times.* Available online. URL: http://www.trussel.com/prehist/news107.htm. Accessed October 8, 2007.

Miller, Stephen A., and John P. Harley. *Zoology, Sixth Edition.* New York: McGraw-Hill, 2005.

National Academy of Sciences. *Science and Creationism: A View from the National Academy of Sciences.* Washington, DC: National Academy of Sciences, 1999.

Palmer, Douglas. *Atlas of the Prehistoric World.* New York: Discovery Books, 1999.

Pearson, Helen. "High Life Prompts Genetic Shift." *Nature News,* February 17, 2004. Available online. URL: http://www.bioedonline. org/news/news.cfm?art=800. Accessed October 8, 2007.

Pitman, Sean D. "Ancient Fossils with Preserved Soft Tissues and DNA." Available online. URL: http://www.naturalselection.0catch.com/Files/ fossilizeddna.html. Accessed October 8, 2007.

Prothero, Donald R., and Robert H. Dott Jr. *Evolution of the Earth.* New York: McGraw-Hill, 2004.

Raup, David M. *Extinction: Bad Genes or Bad Luck?* New York: W.W. Norton, 1991.

———. *The Nemesis Affair.* New York: W.W. Norton, 1986.

Raven, Peter H., George B. Johnson, Jonathan B. Losos, and Susan R. Singer. *Biology, Seventh Edition.* New York: McGraw-Hill, 2005.

Stanley, Steven M. *The New Evolutionary Timetable.* New York: Basic Books, 1981.

University of California Museum of Paleontology. "Fossil Evidence: Transitional Forms" Available online. URL: http://evolution.berkeley. edu/evosite/lines/IAtransitional.shtml. Accessed October 8, 2007.

———. "Introduction to the Bacteria." Available online. URL: http:// www.ucmp.berkeley.edu/bacteria/bacteria.html. Accessed October 8, 2007.

Chapter 6 – How Life is Classified

Blanchette, Mathieu, Eric D. Green, Webb Miller, and David Haussler. "Reconstructing Large Regions of an Ancestral Mammalian Genome in Silico." *Genome Research,* Vol. 14 (2004): 2412–2423.

Fortey, Richard. *Life: A Natural History of the First Four Billion Years of Life on Earth.* New York: Alfred A. Knopf, 1998.

Margulis, Lynn, and Karlene V. Schwartz. *Five Kingdoms: An Illustrated Guide to the Phyla of Life on Earth,* Third Edition. New York: W.H. Freeman, 1998.

Miller, Stephen A., and John P. Harley. *Zoology, Sixth Edition.* New York: McGraw-Hill, 2005.

Raven, Peter H., George B. Johnson, Jonathan B. Losos, and Susan R. Singer. *Biology, Seventh Edition.* New York: McGraw-Hill, 2005.

Woese, Carl R. "The Archaeal Concept And The World It Lives In: A Retrospective." *Photosynthesis Research,* Vol. 80 (2004): 361–372.

———. "Prokaryote Systematics: The Evolution of a Science. *Prokaryotes,* Second Edition. New York, Springer: 1990.

Zwicker, Ken, and TERC. "How Diverse Is Life on Your Site? Taxonomy and the Five Kingdoms of Life." Available online. URL: http://www.concord.org/~btinker/guide/fieldguide/taxonomy.html. Accessed on October 8, 2007.

Chapter 7 – Life's Beginnings

Daniel Y.-C. Wang, Sudhir Kumar, and S. Blair Hedges. "Divergence Time Estimates For The Early History Of Animal Phyla And The Origin Of Plants, Animals And Fungi." *Proceedings of the Royal Society London B,* Vol. 266 (1999): 163–171.

Dunbar, Carl O., and Karl M. Waage. *Historical Geology, Third Edition.* New York: John Wiley & Sons, 1969.

Hopkin, Michael. "Did Volcanoes Help Create Life?" *Nature News.* October 7, 2004. Available online. URL: http://www.bioedonline.org/news/news.cfm?art=1251. Accessed October 8, 2007.

Jun-Yuan Chen, Di-Ying Huang and Chia-Wei Li. "An Early Cambrian Craniate-Like Chordate." *Nature,* Vol. 402 (1999): 518–522.

Morris, Simon Conway. *The Crucible of Creation: The Burgess Shale and the Rise of Animals.* Oxford: Oxford University Press, 1998.

Norman, David. *Prehistoric Life: The Rise of the Vertebrates.* New York: Macmillan, 1994.

Palmer, Douglas. *Atlas of the Prehistoric World.* New York: Discovery Books, 1999.

Prothero, Donald R., and Robert H. Dott Jr. *Evolution of the Earth.* New York: McGraw-Hill, 2004.

Rai, Vibhuti, and Rajita Gautam. "Evaluating Evidence of Ancient Animals." *Science,* Vol 284 (1999): 1235.

University of California Museum of Paleontology. "Vendian Animals: *Tribrachidium.*" Available online. URL: http://www.ucmp.berkeley.edu/vendian/tribrach.html, Accessed October 8, 2007.

Chapter 8 – An Explosion of Life

Budd, Graham E. "A Palaeontological Solution to the Arthropod Head Problem." *Nature,* Vol. 417 (2002): 271–275.

Danley, Patrick D., and Thomas D. Kocher. "Speciation in Rapidly Diverging Systems: Lesson from Lake Malawi." *Molecular Ecology,* Vol. 10 (2001): 1075.

Degan-G. Shu, S. Conway Morris, J. Han, L. Chen, X.-L. Zhang, Z.-F. Zhang, H.-Q. Liu, Y. Li, and J.-N. Liu. "Primitive Deuterostomes from the Chengjiang Lagerstätte (Lower Cambrian, China)." *Nature,* Vol. 414 (2001): 419–424.

Donovan, Stephen K., and David N. Lewis. "The Burgess Shale Biota." *Geology Today,* Vol. 17 (2001): 231–235.

Ellis, Richard. *No Turning Back: The Life and Death of Animal Species.* New York: Harper Collins, 2004.

Gould, Stephen J., editor. *The Book of Life.* New York: W.W. Norton, 1993.

——. *Wonderful Life: The Burgess Shale and the Nature of Mystery.* New York: W.W. Norton, 1989.

Hou X. and J. Bergstrom. "Cambrian Lobopodians-Ancestors Of Extant Onychophorans?" *Zoological Journal of the Linnaean Society,* Vol. 114 (1995): 3–19.

Hughes, C.P. "Redescription of *Burgessia bella* from the Middle Cambrian Burgess Shale, British Columbia." *Fossils and Strata,* No. 4 (1975): 434.

Kirschvink, Joseph L., and Timothy D. Raub. "A Methane Fuse for the Cambrian Explosion: Carbon Cycles and True Polar Wander." *Comptes Rendus Geoscience,* Vol. 335 (2003): 65–78.

Martin, M.W., D.V. Grazhdankin, S.A. Bowring, D.A.D. Evans, M.A. Fedonkin, and J.L. Kirschvink. "Age of Neoproterozoic Bilaterian Body and Trace Fossils, White Sea, Russia: Implications for Metazoan Evolution." *Science,* Vol. 288 (2000): 841–845.

Meyer, Stephen C., P.A. Nelson, and Paul Chien. "The Cambrian Explosion: Biology's Big Bang." Available online. URL: www.geocities. com/mabdulrahmanb/Cambrian.pdf. Accessed on October 8, 2007.

Miller, Stephen A., and John P. Harley. *Zoology, Sixth Edition.* New York: McGraw-Hill, 2005.

Monastersky, Richard. "Mysteries of the Orient—Major Cambrian Fossil Discovery in Chengjiang, China." *Discover.* April 1993. Available online. URL: http://www.findarticles.com/p/articles/mi_m1511/is_n4_v14/ai_13534568. Accessed October 8, 2007.

Morris, Simon Conway. "A New Metazoan From the Cambrian Burgess Shale, British Columbia." *Palaeontology,* Vol. 20 (1977): 623–640.

——. *The Crucible of Creation: The Burgess Shale and the Rise of Animals.* Oxford: Oxford University Press, 1998.

Norman, David. *Prehistoric Life: The Rise of the Vertebrates.* New York: Macmillan, 1994.

Pechenik, Jan A. *Biology of the Invertebrates, Fifth Edition.* New York: McGraw-Hill, 2005.

Peripatus, Chris. "Sirius Passet Lagerstätte." Available online. URL: http://www.peripatus.gen.nz/Paleontology/lagSirPas.html. Accessed October 8, 2007.

Ramsköld, L. "The Second Leg Row Of *Hallucigenia* Discovered." *Lethaia*, Vol. 25 (1992): 221–224.

Smithsonian National Museum of Natural History, Department of Paleobiology. "Burgess Shale Fossil Specimens." Available online. URL: http://paleobiology.si.edu/burgess/burgessSpecimens.html#. Accessed October 8, 2007.

Xian-Guang Hou, Richard J. Aldridge, Jan Bergstrom, David J. Siveter, Derek J. Siveter, and Xiang-Hong Feng. *The Cambrian Fossils of Chengjiang, China: The Flowering of Early Animal Life.* London: Blackwell Publishers, 2004.

FURTHER READING

Gould, Stephen J. *Wonderful Life: The Burgess Shale and the Nature of Mystery*. New York: W.W. Norton, 1989.

Margulis, Lynn, and Karlene V. Schwartz. *Five Kingdoms: An Illustrated Guide to the Phyla of Life on Earth*, Third Edition. New York: W.H. Freeman, 1998.

Morris, Simon Conway. *The Crucible of Creation: The Burgess Shale and the Rise of Animals*. Oxford: Oxford University Press, 1998.

Norman, David. *Prehistoric Life: The Rise of the Vertebrates*. New York: Macmillan, 1994.

Palmer, Douglas. *Atlas of the Prehistoric World*. New York: Discovery Books, 1999.

Taylor, Barbara. *Earth Explained: A Beginner's Guide to Our Planet*. New York: Henry Holt, 1997.

Woese, Carl R. "Prokaryote Systematics: The Evolution of a Science." *Prokaryotes*, Second Edition, New York, Springer, 1990.

Xian-Guang Hou, Richard J. Aldridge, Jan Bergstrom, David J. Siveter, Derek J. Siveter, and Xiang-Hong Feng, *The Cambrian Fossils of Chengjiang, China: The Flowering of Early Animal Life*. London: Blackwell Publishers, 2004.

Web Sites

American Geological Institute: Constructing Understandings of Earth Systems

This extensive site maintained by the American Geological Institute presents information for students, teachers, and the general public on the importance of the geological sciences. The site is comprehensive and clear.

http://www.agiweb.org/education/cues/index.html

American Museum of Natural History: Life Forms

The American Museum of Natural History offers students a colorful exploration of the ocean's bottom-feeding animals.

Kids can learn about a "new world" of life that lives near the hydrothermal vents of the ocean's deep waters.

http://www.amnh.org/nationalcenter/expeditions/blacksmokers/life_forms.html

Kazlev, Alan, and Augustus White: Palaeos: The Trace of Life on Earth

This site provides a broad and detailed exhibition on the basic evolution of life on Earth. Entertaining writing enlivens the scientific discussion of multiple topics.

http://www.palaeos.com/

Maddison, D.R., and K.-S. Schulz. "The Tree of Life Web Project."

Visitors to this site can indulge in a creative exploration of the evolution of living things. The site includes a wealth of information on the world's different species, with images and movies supplementing the text.

http://tolweb.org/tree/phylogeny.html

Peripatus, Chris: Paleontology Page

Easily navigate the detailed history of evolution and paleontology at this site. The site's creator includes several links to other Web pages dedicated to earth science and evolution.

http://www.peripatus.gen.nz/Paleontology/Index.html

Public Broadcasting Service: Evolution Library: Evidence for Evolution

Educational network PBS delivers a comprehensive multimedia site that makes the case for evolution of life on Earth. The site caters to the general public, but offers special features for classroom use.

http://www.pbs.org/wgbh/evolution/library/04/

Scotese, Christopher R.: Paleomap Project

Visitors to this site can browse a large array of maps detailing Earth's geologic changes over time. Animated maps illustrate the site's text. The Earth's climate changes are also discussed.

http://www.scotese.com/

Smithsonian National Museum of Natural History, Department of Paleobiology: Burgess Shale Fossil Specimens

The Smithsonian's department of paleobiology presents graphic illustrations of a variety of fossil specimens. Descriptions of each specimen provide a rounded fossil history.

http://paleobiology.si.edu/burgess/burgessSpecimens.html#

United States Geologic Survey. Inside the Earth

The United States Geologic Survey (USGS) provides an informative lesson on the Earth's interior. Learn about the innermost composition of our planet.

http://pubs.usgs.gov/publications/text/inside.html

University of California Museum of Paleontology: Fossil Evidence: Transitional Forms

If you doubt the theory of evolution, perhaps this site, managed by the University of California Museum of Paleontology, will change your mind. The site presents "transitional forms" of species, or those fossils found between those of the ancient past and those of today.

http://evolution.berkeley.edu/evosite/lines/IAtransitional.shtml

Zwicker, Ken, and TERC: How Diverse Is Life on Your Site? Taxonomy and the Five Kingdoms of Life

This site presents information on taxonomy, or the classification of Earth's myriad life-forms. Students can learn of the specific taxonomic categories and examples of biology that fall under each.

http://www.concord.org/~btinker/guide/fieldguide/taxonomy.html

PICTURE CREDITS

Page

INDEX

ABOUT THE AUTHOR

THOM HOLMES is a writer specializing in natural history subjects and dinosaurs. He is noted for his expertise on the early history of dinosaur science in America. He was the publications director of *The Dinosaur Society* for six years (1991–1997) and the editor of its newsletter, *Dino Times*, the world's only monthly publication devoted to news about dinosaur discoveries. It was through the Society and his work with the Academy of Natural Sciences in Philadelphia that Thom developed widespread contacts and working relationships with paleontologists and paleo-artists throughout the world.

Thom's published works include *Fossil Feud: The Rivalry of America's First Dinosaur Hunters* (Silver Burdett Press, September, 1997); *The Dinosaur Library* (Enslow, 2001-2002); *Duel of the Dinosaur Hunters* (Pearson Education, 2002); *Fossil Feud: The First American Dinosaur Hunters* (Silver Burdett/Julian Messner, 1997). His many honors and awards include the National Science Teachers Association's *Outstanding Science Book of 1998,* VOYA's 1997 Nonfiction Honor List, an Orbis Pictus Honor, and the Chicago Public Library Association's *"Best of the Best"* in science books for young people.

Thom did undergraduate work in geology and studied paleontology through his role as a staff educator with the Academy of Natural Sciences in Philadelphia. He is a regular participant in field exploration, with two recent expeditions to Patagonia in association with Canadian, American, and Argentinian universities.

Made in the USA
Columbia, SC
01 May 2022